END FINANCIAL STRESS

NOW

Immediate Steps You Can Take to
Improve Your Financial Outlook

EMILY GUY BIRKEN

Author of *The 5 Years Before You Retire*

Adams Media
New York London Toronto Sydney New Delhi

Adams Media
An Imprint of Simon & Schuster, Inc.
57 Littlefield Street
Avon, Massachusetts 02322

First Adams Media trade paperback edition MAY 2017

ADAMS MEDIA and colophon are trademarks of Simon and Schuster.

For information about special discounts for bulk purchases, please contact Simon & Schuster Special Sales at 1-866-506-1949 or business@simonandschuster.com.

The Simon & Schuster Speakers Bureau can bring authors to your live event. For more information or to book an event contact the Simon & Schuster Speakers Bureau at 1-866-248-3049 or visit our website at www.simonspeakers.com.

Interior design by Heather McKiel

Manufactured in the United States of America

10 9 8 7 6 5 4 3 2 1

Library of Congress Cataloging-in-Publication Data has been applied for.

ISBN 978-1-4405-9913-2
ISBN 978-1-4405-9914-9 (ebook)

Dedication

For Jayme, who solved my whole DIY dilemma by being a combination of Bob Vila and Jay Leno. Man with tools wins!

Contents

Acknowledgments

This book could not have come to be without the help of many kind and knowledgeable friends and experts:

A particular thank you to my editor Peter Archer, who shows me the error of my grammatical ways with grace and humor. I so enjoy working with you.

Jacqueline Musser of Adams Media encouraged me to write this book. Thank you for giving me the chance to make it happen.

Philip Taylor of PTMoney.com has been an unfailing advocate of my work from day one, when he gave me a chance to write for his site back in November 2010. He was kind enough to allow me to repurpose pieces I wrote for him for this book. Thank you for all that you have done and continue to do.

Thank you to Janet Al-Saad, Amanda Bellucco, Will Chen, Joe Epstein, Chrissa Hardy, Amy Lu, Lars Peterson, William Tran, and Lynn Truong at WiseBread.com who also generously allowed me to use excerpts of articles I had written for them. I have had such fun writing for Wise Bread all these years, guys.

Jeffrey Trull and the editing team at StudentLoanHero.com, as well as David Ning of MoneyNing.com, and Gary Foreman of The Dollar Stretcher also deserve thanks for allowing me to excerpt work I wrote for those sites. I appreciate your help.

Dr. Bradley Klontz allowed me to once again use the money script quiz appearing in Chapter 7. Thank you for being so generous with your time and resources.

A big thank you to my friend Steven Lang, who was kind enough to help me with research on mortgage refinance. You are a true mensch, sir!

My friends Erika Plank Hagan and Marissa Miller kindly allowed me to use some of their personal stories as examples in this book. Yes, I know it's weird that I not only remembered random stories you told me years ago, but that I also got in touch to ask for permission to tell them in a book. That's all part of why you love me, right?

My sister Tracie Guy-Decker is the smartest person I know, and a phone call to her is my surest path through writer's/idea block. Thank you for always being there to talk things through with me.

My mother, Marian Berman, has been telling me behavioral economics stories my whole life—but neither of us knew it. Mom, thanks for teaching me the important role that story plays in demonstrating complex ideas. And for asking me to nod my head yes.

My father, Jim Guy, is no longer with us, but I am thankful for him every day. Dad taught me the importance of aiming for a modest tax refund of $500 or less, along with other arcane rules that helped me understand money better than any other ten-year-old. Thanks for never assuming I was too young to understand, Dad.

Introduction:
The End of Your Money Worries

What if I told you that it was possible to stop worrying about money, forever?

Money is the number one cause of stress for Americans. According to the 2015 American Psychological Association (APA) study "Stress in America," nearly three-quarters of Americans reported feeling stressed about money at least some of the time, and one in four reported experiencing extreme money stress in the past month.

All of this worry is affecting our health. Increased stress leads to unhealthy behaviors, such as excessive screen time, overeating, smoking, and drinking. With many Americans putting their healthcare needs on the back burner when financial worries loom, the money-stress-illness cycle becomes even more entrenched.

It would be bad enough if worrying about money just affected the worrier, but financial stress is also ruining marriages. A 2012 study of 4,500 married couples revealed that fighting about money is the biggest predictor of divorce—and, of course, divorce doesn't do much to help either spouse's bottom line.

Marriage is not the only relationship that money stress can hurt. According to a 2012 study of college students' financial behaviors, children of parents who fight about money are reportedly more likely to struggle with credit card debt as young adults. And even if the children of money-stressed parents are not destined to fall into a debt trap, financial arguments at home can teach kids that money is a fraught and negative topic, making it more difficult for them to learn healthy financial behaviors.

All in all, just thinking about money is enough to give you an ulcer.

But—at the risk of repeating myself—suppose you could stop worrying about money, forever?

Changing Your Relationship with Money

No, I'm not offering advice on how to win the lottery, make a killing on the stock market, or befriend a doddering multimillionaire. Even if you were to follow any of those "paths" to riches, it would not end your worries about finances. You only have to look at the scores of lottery winners who have gone bankrupt to know that having pots of money is not the answer to ending financial woes.

In fact, when I talk about ending money stress, I am not even referring to that common goal of achieving "financial security"—the elusive sense that you have enough money to survive any financial catastrophe.

That's because I believe the entire idea of financial security is an illusion. There is always a potential catastrophe that could wipe out any fortune, no matter how big.

As frightening as the impossibility of financial security is, I am here to tell you that money does not need to be a source of worry, stress, or strife. You can make your peace with money, fulfill all of your financial obligations, and feel much more contented—at any income.

Think it sounds too good to be true? It's not.

What I will teach you to do is change your outlook on money. Instead of aiming for the ever-moving goal of financial security, where you feel that your money can handle any catastrophe, you will learn to change your attitude and recognize that you can handle whatever financial hurdles life throws at you.

Once you have changed your attitude toward money, your money stress will lessen. That's because you will feel in control of your life, rather than believing that your money is behind the wheel.

Letting Go of Financial Stress

This book will teach you how to reframe your view of your current financial situation and adjust your attitude toward money in general.

- You will learn how to get more satisfaction out of your purchases, your work, and your life.
- You will discover the universal economic and behavioral problems that make it difficult to be rational about money.
- You will explore your own psychological money makeup, and you will learn how to work within that mental framework instead of against it.
- And you will be given a road map for creating a fulfilling financial life that is free of stress.

The book is broken into the following four parts and applying each one will help you end your financial stress:

PART ONE: Redefining Money

This portion of the book will help you to understand that money and value are not synonymous. In Chapters 1 through 3, we will discuss the nature of currency, the common mistake of discounting nonfinancial costs, and the types of illusions we all share about money.

PART TWO: Economic Reasons Why We Struggle with Money

The second portion of the book will introduce you to several principles of economic theory that can help you understand why some financial problems are so common. Chapter 4 will introduce you to the surprising consequences of living with scarcity. In Chapter 5, you will learn about the various ways our brains are wired to make us bad with money. Chapter 6 will explore how our fear of losing what we have can lead to self-sabotaging money mistakes.

PART THREE: Psychological Reasons Why You Struggle with Money

This section of the book will help you identify the personal obstacles that keep you from achieving your financial goals. Chapters 7 and 8 will help you identify the money lessons you picked up in childhood and explore some techniques for unlearning harmful beliefs and habits. Chapter 9 will help you to examine the mental hurdles in your path and establish workarounds for them.

PART FOUR: Achieving a Stress-Free Financial Life

The final four chapters of the book will help you create a road map for achieving a stress-free financial life, based upon your specific circumstances and temperament. Chapter 10 offers actionable ways for you to build financial breathing room into your budget. In Chapter 11, we will go over several budgeting methods so you can find a process that will work for you. Chapter 12 offers you ways to improve your self-regulation and self-discipline, so that financial temptations become less alluring. Finally, Chapter 13 will help you deal with resentment, one of the most tenacious negative emotions surrounding money.

Money Doesn't Have to Be Stressful

You can feel better about money, no matter where you are financially. This book will teach you the skills you need to transform your relationship with money without making drastic changes to your income.

Let's end your financial worries for good.

Note to the Reader

One of the biggest criticisms of books of financial advice is that they often assume a minimum level of income or upward mobility. Individuals who are stuck in a cycle of poverty can be forgiven for assuming that advice written by a privileged personal finance expert will not apply to them.

I want to make it clear to my readers that I am fully aware of the overwhelming systemic financial issues that affect many people. The sad fact is that financial disenfranchisement of various groups has been a consistent part of our economy from the beginning, and the idea that anyone can bootstrap herself out of poverty with enough grit is the inspiring picture we have painted over the truth.

In fact, truly bootstrapping oneself from poverty to wealth is exceedingly rare, because it takes a nearly inhuman level of perfect financial behavior to achieve it. For most people, real life is messy and imperfect, and financial mistakes are par for the course. All of this can be enough to make many people either give up or turn to get-rich-quick schemes when they feel ground down by the very real problems of systemic poverty.

That's why I wrote this book. Unlike others of its kind, *End Financial Stress Now* will not ask for perfect behavior from you, nor does it promise you an end to all financial *problems*. Applying the advice in this book to your life will help ease your money worries, even if you are dealing with systemic poverty or financial distress that is not of your making.

The advice in this book cannot fix the systemic problems that continually leave many of our citizens impoverished. Those problems can only be fixed on the societal level. However, this book does offer strategies for financial stress relief to any and all readers who are willing to try them, no matter their financial situation. While we work together as a society to level the playing field, you can do the work that will help you feel more confident and peaceful about your own financial situation.

Let's roll up our sleeves and get started.

PART ONE

Redefining Money

We rarely take the time to really think about what money is, what it means, and how we use it. This is especially troubling because many of us have faulty assumptions about money. This section examines the ways that we value and assign meaning to money, and you will learn how those valuations and meanings may lead you to make poor financial decisions.

CHAPTER ONE

What Does Money Mean to You?

WHAT YOU'LL LEARN IN THIS CHAPTER

- The rational view of money described by classical economic theory is overly idealistic, although it can still be of some use.
- When we assign emotional meanings to money, those meanings can cause us to act irrationally.
- When you identify the emotional meaning money has for you, you can better understand some of the ways that you might act against your own financial self-interest.

According to classical economic theory, human beings are rational economic agents who always make the best choices for their own self-interest. Such a rational individual—dubbed *homo economicus* by economists in the late nineteenth century—always has the full information necessary to make cost-benefit analyses on any particular financial matter, from determining if a car's expensive repair is worth the money to knowing where to invest retirement funds. *Homo economicus* is never caught flatfooted by any financial decisions, and he is able to methodically and logically maximize the bang for his buck in every situation. He never puts off financial decisions, never spends money for emotional reasons, never holds on to depreciating assets, never invests in terrible business ideas, never pays more than what something is worth, never gives money to untrustworthy relatives or friends, never throws good money after bad, never buys a latte when he can brew his own coffee, and he never makes any mistakes.

He's kind of a jerk, actually.

However, it's heartening to learn that the field of behavioral economics has determined that homo economicus is more myth than reality. Behavioral economists, who study how people react to economic situations in the real world, have shown again and again through experiments and observation that human beings simply do not have the ability to separate their emotions from financial transactions. In an ideal world of classical economic theory, human beings behave with unyielding rationality; but in the real world, human beings are irrational, emotional, and easily overwhelmed.

Despite the fact that the idealized figure of homo economicus is about as realistic as the tooth fairy, there is something that we mere mortals can learn from this model. In fact, learning to be more like a rational person is one of the things you can do to help ease your financial stress.

That's because the rational homo economicus does not feel stressed when faced with difficult financial decisions. Nor does he overreact to financial stress triggers. Instead, he weighs his options and chooses the one that will maximize his money, time, or utility. Though no human being will ever become the completely emotionless robot that classical economic theory assumes the ideal worker and consumer to be, we can work to put some space between our finances and how we feel about our finances. When we can provide even a little separation between our emotions and our financial decisions, we can be better able to both improve our financial decision-making skills and gain some much-needed financial stress relief.

To create this necessary space, we need to start with an understanding of the various things that money means, beyond just dollars and cents.

What Does Money Mean?

If I were to ask you to write a comprehensive and universal definition of money, you would probably be annoyed at me for giving you an essay question as homework—and you might feel a little flummoxed by the task. That's because money is maddeningly difficult to quantify. Even though it is a mundane part of our everyday lives and something that affects every one of us, money is ultimately nothing more than a huge and amorphous idea that we all share.

Here is the truth: Money is valuable, but that is only because we have all agreed that it is valuable. You cannot eat money, wear money, build shelter out of money, or even spend your money outside of the places that accept it as legal tender. Its value lies solely in our social agreement about its value.

This means money takes on the philosophical, psychological, emotional, and moral meanings that we assign to it, which are hardly universal. Often it is these assigned meanings that direct our choices rather than the deep thought or the rational cost-benefit analyses that are necessary to come to the best decision. Here are several of the common meanings you may associate with money.

MONEY IS A SOURCE OF SHAME

Money is morally neutral, despite the oft-misquoted Bible verse about money's relationship to evil. (The actual quotation from Timothy 6:10 is "The love of money is a root of all kinds of evil.") Being without money is neither a good nor a bad thing, just as having money is neither a good nor a bad thing. It just is.

Yet, we have a tendency to moralize money, poverty, and wealth, and we therefore experience shame in relationship to money. As a society, we often vilify the impoverished (and the wealthy), as if their morality is tied to their net worth. Those without money often feel shame—and are sometimes shamed—for their situation.

This shame manifests itself in poor decisions. For instance, someone who feels ashamed of her lack of resources might avoid opportunities to better her situation, such as budgeting/finance classes at her church or financial aid seminars offered by her local community college. Her shame at not having money and needing help can keep her stuck in the same financial position.

MONEY IS RESPECT

Money merely represents the amount of goods and services its possessor can purchase, but many of us assume a thick wallet means greater respect. There is a good reason for this assumption: When you appear to be wealthy, daily interactions with strangers do tend to be more respectful.

For instance, when I was a student teacher in 2006, I dropped by a local mall after school one afternoon in order to buy a gift for my cooperating teacher. I was dressed professionally and carrying a briefcase—and every single salesperson I passed attempted to get my attention and called me "ma'am." I was given much prompter service than I was used to in the store where I bought the gift. But other than the thirty bucks I had already set aside to spend on the specific gift I had come to buy, I had no money whatsoever to spare. In fact, since I was living on savings and a student loan and paying for the opportunity to student teach, I was in pretty dire financial straits. My professional clothing just gave me the illusion of wealth.

That kind of illusory respect can be enticing to anyone who does not feel respected elsewhere in his life. Such a person might get into debt in order to appear wealthier than he is, just to experience the sense of respect that the appearance of money offers him.

MONEY IS SECURITY

Living without enough money is a nerve-racking and crazy-making experience, wherein you feel at all times as if the rug can be pulled out from underneath your life. Individuals who see money as security believe that having more money will provide them with the sense of safety they need. For some such individuals, spending any money—even on necessary items or services—can seem foolhardy, because it is eating into their security.

While it is true that living without much money can be an insecure existence, money itself cannot provide security. That's partially because there is no specific amount of money that can offer complete and total financial security in the face of certain problems. Although the fear underlying this belief system may have a rational motivation—the desire to avoid living from hand-to-mouth—it can be applied irrationally. Individuals who believe money is security might be afraid to spend money on higher education or to start a business, even though those expenditures could greatly improve their lives.

MONEY IS FREEDOM

Anyone who has ever hated her job or felt stuck in a terrible relationship because she couldn't otherwise afford the rent has experienced the sense that more money buys freedom. The lifestyle available to someone who does not have to work for a living or who does not have to rely on others to get by certainly does look like freedom to anyone stuck in untenable positions. A sudden influx of cash would allow you to tell your boss, your boyfriend, or your landlord where to stuff it, and provide you with the opportunity to live the life you really want.

But even though that sounds very much like freedom, it's actually just "options." Money does not truly buy freedom—but the more of it you have, the more choices you have available to you. When your life feels constricted it's perfectly rational to dream of the greater options money could give you.

Unfortunately, believing that money offers freedom can lead to any number of irrational financial behaviors, including susceptibility to get-rich-quick schemes, gambling, indebtedness, and even hoarding.

MONEY IS SUCCESS

Other than recognition, money is often the only indicator of success that we can all agree upon as a society. If a professional is making good money, we describe him as successful, even if he is miserable in his job. The money is the marker for success, and his life satisfaction does not come into the conversation.

As with many other money beliefs, believing that money equals success has some merit. According to the social agreement, our economy is nominally set up as a meritocracy, wherein the free market awards money to those who are most successful. Make the best product and/or offer the best services, and you will be rewarded with the most money.

While there is a grain of truth to this idea, it does not reflect the whole of what it means to be successful.

This belief can be problematic since it ignores the aspects of a successful life that offer no financial reward, such as strong, positive relationships. Individuals who believe that money is success may be prone to workaholism, and as a consequence may neglect their nonprofessional relationships. They may chase dollar signs without enjoying any part of the journey.

MONEY IS LOVE

Being able to financially take care of your family can be a major point of pride for many people. In many cases, that's because money is equivalent to love. For these individuals, the surest way to show their family love is to provide for them financially—with anything from the latest toys and clothes to private school tuition to family vacations to a beautiful home to lavish gifts.

The problem with this belief is the fact that many family members would prefer to spend time with the overworked individuals whose bank balances may be full of love, but who leave an empty spot at the dinner table every night. Believing money is love also leaves such individuals feeling unlovable if they lose their jobs or are unable to provide at a certain level.

MONEY IS TIME

The old saying may be "time is money," but if you have ever worked multiple jobs to make ends meet, then you know that the opposite is true. Though money and time are both finite resources, time is the only resource that is allocated evenly—every person receives the same twenty-four hours in each day. However, individuals with more money are able to use their time more efficiently by spending money to save time.

For instance, a 2014 study found that commuters in five major U.S. cities wait approximately forty minutes per day for public transportation—which adds up to 150 hours per year. Having enough money to afford a car would free up that time for those commuters, meaning they could spend those 150 hours per year doing something they like better than waiting for a bus or train to arrive.

Believing that money equals time is eminently reasonable. In most transactions, you will either have to spend money or spend time in order to get what you want. That is, for dinner you could pay for burgers and fries at the Golden Arches, or you could spend time (and less money) grocery shopping, cooking, and cleaning up. The problem is that many of the financially poor are also time poor, meaning they cannot easily get ahead with either currency.

Living with this financial belief can lead to shortcuts in order to try to save time. For example, a time- and money-crunched individual might buy a cheap car to reduce her public transportation wait time, only to find that her inexpensive car needs pricey repairs, costing her even more time and more money.

Figuring Out What Money Means to You

Just reading through the common beliefs that we assign to money can be an eye-opening experience because our beliefs surrounding money tend to reside outside of our awareness. Recognizing yourself in any of the previous belief systems can be incredibly helpful, but if you want to build up some real space between your beliefs about money and your reactions to money, then you will need to dig a little deeper. It starts with a fun exercise: figuring out what you would do if you suddenly received $1 million. Answer the following question quickly and without thinking too hard about it. The goal is to access your gut reaction to the idea of sudden wealth.

If I had $1 million, the first thing I would buy would be:

....

Answering this question can either be a fun way to daydream or a frustrating exercise in remembering what you don't have. Either way, probing a little deeper into your immediate reaction to a sudden windfall will help you to better understand what you feel about money.

The Five Whys

Let's dig into what your $1 million response means about your money beliefs. A great way to do this is by using a tool borrowed from the world of engineering, known as the Five Whys. This tool, which author and blogger Ramit Sethi of the site *I Will Teach You to Be Rich* (www.iwillteachyoutoberich.com) recommends for diagnosing personal finance problems, was originally developed by Sakichi Toyoda of the Toyota Motor Corporation in order to help diagnose the root causes of engineering problems. In the automotive world, a Five Whys technique might look like this example from Wikipedia:

- Problem: The vehicle will not start.
- Why? The battery is dead. (First why.)
- Why? The alternator is not functioning. (Second why.)
- Why? The alternator belt has broken. (Third why.)
- Why? The alternator belt was well beyond its useful service life and not replaced. (Fourth why.)
- Why? The vehicle was not maintained according to the recommended service schedule. (Fifth why, and the root cause.)

In our case, instead of trying to find the root cause of an engineering problem, we are going to try to figure out what emotional issues are at the root of our beliefs about money. In addition, we are not starting with a problem, per se, but with our preferences about money. It may also take less than the full five whys to come to the emotional root of our money preferences. Let's look at an example:

- If I had $1 million, the first thing I would buy would be a whole new wardrobe.
- Why? I hate dressing in hand-me-downs or castoffs.
- Why? Wearing used clothes makes me feel invisible.
- Why? I had to wear castoffs when I was a kid, and no one wanted to talk to me.

In this example, it only took three whys to understand that the emotional meaning of money is acceptance and connection. This woman feels invisible and sees money as a method of being accepted, since wearing secondhand clothes as a child meant she felt like an outcast. Once she recognizes that she craves a sense of acceptance and connection, she can start doing the work necessary to provide herself with it. In addition, she will be in a better position to recognize that money will not make her feel accepted, no matter how many wardrobes it can buy her.

Now it's your turn. Copy down your answer to the previous $1 million question, and quickly answer the Five Whys. By the time you reach your fifth why (or perhaps earlier), you'll likely understand the emotional need that you want money to fill.

Worksheet 1-1: The Five Whys

- If I had $1 million, the first thing I would buy would be:
....
- Why? ....
- Why? ....
- Why? ....
- Why? ....
- Why? ....

Now that you have identified some of the emotional meaning you have assigned to money, you'll be in a better position to meet those emotional needs outside of your financial decisions.

Of course, this is hardly an easy prospect. Identifying and satisfying your unmet emotional needs can be the work of a lifetime—and it is certainly beyond the scope of this book. However, simply being aware of your emotional reaction to money can be a great start toward improving your relationship with money. If you know the emotional need you are trying to fill with money, you can take the time to ask yourself if the financial choice you are about to make will actually fulfill that need. That little bit of space between your knee-jerk emotional reaction and the actual financial decision you make can be enough to help you emulate *homo economicus*, and reduce your financial stress.

Chapter One Takeaways

1. Classical economic theory expects all individuals to behave rationally, even though more recent studies by behavioral economists have proven that human beings cannot separate emotions from money.

2. Though money is universal, the emotional meanings we have assigned to it are not.

3. Some common meanings assigned to money include the idea that money is a source of shame, money is respect, money is security, money is freedom, money is success, money is love, and money is time.

4. Identifying the emotional meaning you have assigned to money can provide you with enough space between your emotions and your financial decisions to help you make better choices.

CHAPTER TWO

Understanding Opportunity Cost

WHAT YOU'LL LEARN IN THIS CHAPTER

- An important aspect of ending financial stress is recognizing all of the costs associated with financial transactions. Our tendency to consider only purely monetary costs in any particular transaction obscures its true cost.
- Opportunity cost is the value of whatever you give up when you make any decision.
- It is easy to ignore or incorrectly value opportunity costs.
- Free (and inexpensive) items can often end up costing us more.
- The sunk cost fallacy can cause us to waste money and time.
- Misvaluing opportunity costs can cause financial difficulties.

Every decision you make requires you to forgo whatever options you didn't choose. This phenomenon is called opportunity cost, and ignoring it can have huge consequences on both your finances and your stress level.

In the simplest terms, an opportunity cost is the value of whatever you give up in order to do something. For instance, spending $8 on lunch means you cannot spend that $8 on anything else. The opportunity cost of that $8 burger is the value of whatever else you might have done with the money—whether that something else is buying a cup of coffee and a muffin the next morning or putting an additional $8 in your savings account.

Opportunity costs can be easy to recognize when you know exactly what you are giving up when you spend your money. If you've got your eye on the new iPhone but have to pay rent, you know that spending $500 on rent means giving up that newest Apple gadget.

The concept of opportunity cost becomes more complex when you have to consider nonfinancial things you might be giving up. For instance, watching television all afternoon may cost you nothing financially, but it costs you whatever else you could have done with that time.

My Real World Introduction to Opportunity Cost

One of my first jobs was working as an administrative assistant for the main office of a small chain of franchised restaurants. The owner walked by my desk one morning and noticed that I had an entire drawer full of rubber bands. The collection had already been there when I started the job, and being of a frugal nature, I continued to save the rubber bands that came in with the weekly paperwork from each of the stores in our chain. My boss remarked that he hated to think of the managers wasting money by buying new rubber bands, and could I please package them up and send them out to the dozen stores. He was so unhappy with the idea of paying money for rubber bands that it did not occur to him that it cost him more money to pay me for the chore, not to mention the price of packaging and transportation to the stores, and the time cost of having me repackage rubber bands for an hour when there was plenty of other work for me to do. It was the first time I truly understood the phrase "spending a dollar to save a nickel."

In many cases, opportunity costs are very clear. For instance, if you have ever waffled between two similarly priced entrees on a restaurant menu, then you have considered your opportunity costs. You know that picking the chicken over the pasta means giving up the enjoyment of eating that pasta, which is precisely why it can be so difficult to decide. By picking the chicken, you are taking the risk that the pasta might have been tastier.

Every transaction is a trade-off between the benefit and the opportunity cost. It's easy to see what the benefit and opportunity costs might be when choosing between the chicken and the pasta, but many of your regular transactions have much more opaque or abstract trade-offs.

In particular, when you get something for free, you tend to ignore all of the potential opportunity costs to the transaction. This can actually lead to "free" costing you money.

Why It May Cost You More When It's Free

There is a point in the raunchy 2001 comedy *Super Troopers* when the brain trust of the group, Farva, is filling up his car with gas. He notices a sign at the gas station advertising a free hot dog with a ten-gallon fill up. Farva is disappointed when his fill up comes to just over nine gallons, so he empties nearly a gallon of gas into a trash can so he can get his free hot dog. He is so focused on the "free" hot dog that he doesn't realize it would probably cost him less overall to just buy a hot dog on top of his nine-gallon fill up.

I remember thinking, "What an idiot!" while I giggled at the movie. Yet, I (and everyone else) tend to be just as big of an idiot when the word "free" is bandied about.

Just think about the last time you needed to buy something from Amazon. If it was a purchase under the free-shipping threshold, the retail giant helpfully informed you that just adding $X to your order qualified you for free shipping. So, in order to save yourself around $4 in shipping costs, you made an impulse purchase that ended up costing more than what you were saving. I've certainly done it, and I'm likely to do it again—as are you. Deep down, we're not so different from the gas-squandering Farva because we have trouble recognizing opportunity costs when something is free.

THE WORD "FREE" CAN CHANGE YOUR BEHAVIOR

You don't have to look far to find examples of free offers that make people act in ways they normally don't. For example, even the most clutter-averse individual will find it difficult to turn down free items offered at conferences or banking offices. Similarly, "free gifts with purchase" can sometimes be enough of an enticement to convince an on-the-fence shopper to make a purchase. In my own life, I remember being unsure whether I really wanted or needed a new blouse—but being convinced that I really ought to buy it because a second one was free.

Dan Ariely, behavioral economist and author of the book *Predictably Irrational*, observed a promotion in New York City that drives home the reality of how the concept of "free" can scramble our ability to recognize opportunity costs.

A nightclub offered patrons free tattoos for attending an event, so Ariely and his team decided to interview the patrons opting for these tattoos. Fifty-two of the seventy-six people in line for the free tattoo said they would not be getting the tattoo if it were not free—which is pretty startling considering that we are talking about permanent body modification. In addition, four of the people in line for the tattoos didn't even know what design they wanted, and an additional five did not know where they wanted their new ink.

As the tattoo example illustrates, the concept of "free" affects our behavior. Presumably, fifty-two people in line that night would be tattooless if they hadn't been offered free tattoos.

Why on earth does the word "free" have such a strange effect on our minds? You can be relatively certain that had the nightclub been offering $1 tattoos rather than free ones, there would not have been seventy-six people in line—and certainly not individuals who didn't even know what ink they wanted. A $1 tattoo is an incredible deal, but as compared to free it's less of an enticement to change behavior.

According to Ariely, the issue comes down to a fear of loss. He describes this fear in *Predictably Irrational*:

Most transactions have an upside [benefit] and a downside [opportunity cost], but when something is free we forget the downside. Free gives us such an emotional charge that we perceive what is being offered as immensely more valuable than it really is. Why? I think it's because humans are intrinsically afraid of loss. The real allure of free is tied to this fear. There's no visible possibility of loss when we choose a free item (it's free). But suppose we chose the item that's *not* free. Uh-oh, now there's a risk of having made a poor decision—the possibility of a loss.

Avoiding this fear of possible loss makes free items seem much more attractive than they really are. After all, we think that there's no way to lose money on the free item—and losing money is usually the downside or opportunity cost of any transaction. Without the explicit loss of money, we think of the transaction as only having an upside or positive outcome for us.

THE COST OF FREE

Of course, just because a transaction is financially free (or just because it *feels* free, which was Farva's downfall) does not mean that it is without costs.

For instance, returning to the night of the free tattoos, a competing tattoo artist happened to be at the nightclub, observing the proceedings. She told Ariely's research assistant that the tattoo artist giving the free tattoos was engaging in unhygienic and potentially hazardous cleaning and health practices—and that the artist did not appear to be using any disinfectant. Considering that getting a tattoo can potentially expose you to blood-borne diseases including hepatitis and HIV, the possible cost of getting a tattoo can be much more than the amount of money you hand over to the artist.

That is the sort of opportunity cost that many of us are unable to recognize when we are dazzled by the word "free." It pays to really think through the consequences of a free offer before enthusiastically signing up.

Sunk Cost versus Opportunity Cost

A sunk cost is the time, money, or resources that have already been spent, and cannot be recouped, on a project or goal. Sunk costs should have no bearing on whether or not you continue with a project, because the money has already been spent and cannot in any way affect the outcome.

However, something called the sunk cost fallacy is a big reason why many people are unable to give up on a lost cause. According to Stephen J. Dubner, of *Freakonomics* fame, "The sunk cost fallacy is when you tell yourself that you can't quit because of all that time or money you spent. We shouldn't fall for this fallacy, but we do it all the time."

For instance, a newly minted doctor who realizes during his first year of residency that medicine is no longer the career he wants might stick with it anyway to keep from wasting all of that time he spent in school. What he fails to recognize is that the time was "wasted" anyway, since he doesn't want to be a doctor. Becoming a doctor now will be wasting even more time because he'll be following a path he is not interested in.

This is similar to the common reason many people give for not going back to school in adulthood to train for their dream career. A person might say, "I'll be fifty-two years old by the time I get my degree and can start looking for jobs in that field—it's too late for me." This "logic" ignores the fact that the speaker will be fifty-two years old on that date regardless of whether or not she goes back to school. If she really wants the degree, she might as well enroll and move toward a future wherein she is a fifty-two-year-old with her chosen degree rather than a fifty-two-year-old with more regrets.

We all experience the sunk cost fallacy on an almost daily basis. For instance, let's say you bought a nonrefundable ticket for a concert but come down with the flu on the day of the event. You might force yourself to go to the concert instead of doing what you'd prefer—resting at home—for fear of "wasting" the money you spent on the ticket. That money is a sunk cost. The money is gone whether you go to the concert and sneeze through three sets or you go home and get the rest you need.

Similarly, you might decide to continue watching a movie you hate because you don't want to waste the money or time you've already put into it. Or you might continue to go to the eight-week fitness class you paid for in advance even though you realized after one class that you hate it with a rare and overwhelming passion.

In each of these cases, from the life-changing to the mundane, the sunk costs should not be a factor in your future choices. The only costs you should consider are opportunity costs. Those are the costs of continuing along your current path. For every dollar or hour or resource you spend in any endeavor, you have one less to spend elsewhere.

Our hypothetical doctor should consider the opportunity cost of finishing his residency: He will have less time to do what he really loves. When he looks at the possibility of quitting in that way, it is clearer that becoming a doctor will cost him much more than just the time he has already wasted.

On the smaller scale, you should think about what you really want to do with your time or money and not focus on the money and/or time you have already spent and cannot recoup.

Misvaluing Opportunity Costs

In many cases, people tend to ignore or undervalue opportunity costs. Free (or very inexpensive) items can make you forget that there is still a cost to those transactions, and sunk costs can make you discount your opportunity costs.

It is also very common for people to overvalue opportunity costs in some situations, which can lead to stressful and disordered financial behavior. In particular, individuals who have difficulty making up their minds in any transaction are often overvaluing opportunity costs, at the expense of enjoying what they have.

LOOKING FOR THE IDEAL

Imagine you are in the market for a new camera. You carefully research your options, reading through *Consumer Reports* articles and photography forums online, and you ask every amateur photographer you meet which camera he or she considers to be the best. After months of research, you finally pull the trigger on your new purchase.

At the same time, your cousin also decides to buy a new camera. He walks into the nearest camera store and asks for a recommendation from the staff for a good camera within his price range. He walks out with the same model that you bought after less than half an hour in the store.

Who do you suppose will be happier with their purchase?

Psychologists have found that the nonresearched purchase will provide the owner with far more satisfaction than the meticulously researched one. According to Barry Schwartz, author of the book *The Paradox of Choice*, the reason for this has to do with the amount of anxiety you feel during your purchase. The type of person who researches every single feature of a purchase will worry, even after the sale, that there is a better option out there somewhere. He is overvaluing the opportunity cost and making himself a nervous wreck.

Schwartz refers to these buyers as "maximizers." They are attempting to maximize their choices, which seems like a good thing. However, by thinking that there is some sort of ideal version of the item out there, maximizers second-guess their purchase and always worry that they did not get the absolute best, even when they should be enjoying (or at least making peace with) their decision.

Their nonresearching cousins, on the other hand, Schwartz calls "satisficers." Satisficers decide which features of the purchase or decision are most important, and then they stop looking as soon as they find something that meets those criteria. Because they are willing to accept "good enough," they don't feel the need to worry that there is a better option available somewhere. There may well be something better, but it doesn't matter because what they chose is good enough. There is no need to consider and reconsider the choices not taken. Yes, they may have some opportunity cost by making the choice that they made, but that does not stop them from enjoying what they have.

Learning to Become a Satisficer

I have been a satisficer for most of my life, but I wasn't always one. I can pinpoint the moment when I changed from maximizing to satisficing. That moment occurred when I was a child. One day, my father took my sister, my cousin, and me to the toy store so we could each pick out a toy for ourselves. I was torn between the Snoopy Sno-cone Machine and another toy that I simply do not remember.

I took so long pacing between these two toys that my father finally told me (through gritted teeth) to decide immediately or go home with nothing. Forced to choose, I opted for the toy that wasn't the Snoopy Sno-cone Machine. I have no memory of the toy I chose that day, but I can still describe to the last detail the Snoopy Sno-cone Machine. That's because I overvalued the Snoopy toy—it was my opportunity cost for choosing the other toy.

Since I clearly did not get my father's money's worth of enjoyment out of the other toy, what with all the Snoopy Sno-cone pining I did over the years, I learned to stop being so particular and start making decisions that were practical and based on less stringent criteria.

Opportunity Cost and Regret

Whether you are undervaluing or overvaluing opportunity cost in any transaction, your misevaluation of opportunity cost is generally an attempt to avoid regret. Forgetting to factor in opportunity costs in free transactions stems from a fear of regret—we jump at a free offer because we assume there will be nothing to regret when we pay nothing. Falling for the sunk cost fallacy has a similar basis, wherein we are afraid we will regret the fact that we have "wasted" money or time and ignore the possibility that we might regret wasting even more money and time. Searching for the best, most ideal option is an attempt to stave off the regret we might feel for making the wrong choice.

In all of these cases, however, trying to avoid regret often lands you in a big steaming pile of it.

Appropriately valuing opportunity cost so that you neither under- nor overthink your transactions and feel satisfied with your choices is not an easy feat. However, there are some mental tricks you can use to combat the tendency to misevaluate opportunity costs.

COMBATTING THE EFFECT OF FREE

Here are some ways you can avoid falling for the free fallacy.

Do Not Accept Anything for Free That You Wouldn't Pay For

A friend of mine is a master crafter who homeschools her two chil- dren. They have a local thrift store that offers great art supplies for pen- nies on the dollar. My friend, however, only buys things at the thrift store that she'd be willing to pay full price for. That may seem counter- intuitive, but that helps her to remember to buy only things she'll really use, rather than stuff that's just cheap.

This brilliant strategy for thrift store finds works equally well for free items. Just say no to free things (whether they're tattoos at a night- club or yet another coffee mug at your next conference) unless you would be willing to spend the money on them.

Imagine a Free Item Costs Fifty Cents

Dan Ariely also suggests that consumers imagine their free-with- purchase item (whether it's a hot dog or shipping) actually costs fifty cents. If it doesn't seem like as good a deal then, it will be much easier to walk away.

COMBATTING THE SUNK COST FALLACY

Ignoring sunk costs is tough, but these thought exercises can help you remember that your opportunity costs are more important.

Imagine You Just Woke Up with Amnesia

Luciano Passuello, blogger at Litemind (https://litemind.com), came up with the term "zero-based thinking" to describe this method of combatting the sunk cost fallacy. Passuello suggests you act as though all you have is the present. You can do this by imagining you just woke up in your current situation with amnesia; you have no idea how you got there. That allows your current decision to reside wholly in the present, rather than focusing on what sunk costs will be "lost" by making any decision.

Proudly Admit Your Mistakes

Philosophy graduate student Ryan Doody at MIT wrote a chapter of his PhD thesis on the reasons underlying the sunk cost fallacy. He concluded that the pressure to honor sunk costs stems from a desire to hide the fact that you have made a mistake. You may have initially intended to become a doctor (or go to a concert) and even put money and time where your intentions were—but as of right now, you have changed your mind. Ignoring your opportunity costs and continuing along your current path, either to a career in medicine or a miserable night out, will hide the fact that you now feel as though you made a mistake initially and have wasted money and/or time.

If you are willing to proudly admit to your mistakes, no matter how big or small, then the pressure to honor sunk costs will lessen. You can even take some pride in the fact that your willingness to admit to mistakes allows you to make more rational and satisfying choices for yourself.

COMBATTING MAXIMIZING BEHAVIOR

Maximizing behavior can be tough to avoid, but it is possible to research your choices without becoming bogged down by the decision-making process and without second-guessing yourself once you have made your decision.

Use the Three-Then-Five Rule

Searching for the ideal option in any decision is overwhelming if you have all possible options available. Instead, you can create an artificial limit to your choices. Start with three options and compare them in detail. Once you have determined which one of those three is the best, look at up to five more options to compare with the best out of three. If there is an option among the five that is better than the best of the three, choose that. Otherwise, go back to the best of the three. This method will help you feel as though you have done your due diligence to find an option that is as close to optimal as possible without triggering choice overload.

Give Yourself a Time Limit

If you feel the need to learn about every aspect of a decision, it might seem as though you will have to spend the rest of your life engaged in research. Deciding ahead of time that you will make the best choice you can after committing to one hour of research can help to make the decision-making process more doable. If, after your hour of research is up, you still do not feel comfortable making a decision, you can decide to extend your research by another hour—but no more. Giving yourself a time limit can help you remember that you do not need to become the foremost authority in the subject you are researching—you simply need to find an option that will work well enough for your needs.

Chapter Two Takeaways

1. Opportunity cost is the value of whatever options you forgo by making a decision. Choosing to spend $8 on a burger has the opportunity cost of spending that same money on coffee and a muffin.

2. People tend to ignore, undervalue, and overvalue opportunity costs because they are often opaque or abstract.

3. Being offered something for free can often cause consumers to completely ignore potential opportunity costs. We tend to believe that if something is free, then it is without any downsides.

4. Sunk costs are the money, time, or resources that have already been spent and cannot be recouped.

5. The sunk cost fallacy causes people to undervalue opportunity costs in favor of sunk costs, for fear of wasting the money, time, or resources that have already been spent.

6. Overvaluing opportunity cost often manifests in searching for an ideal option, which can lead to dissatisfaction with the decision and second-guessing of your choices.

7. It is possible to appropriately value opportunity costs by using various mental tricks to reach the most rational and satisfying decisions for yourself.

CHAPTER THREE

Understanding Your Mental Accounting

WHAT YOU'LL LEARN IN THIS CHAPTER

- Any dollar in your possession can buy the same amount of goods as any other dollar.
- Some common mental accounting errors often lead to counterproductive financial behaviors.
- You can use your mental accounting to improve your bottom line.
- You can recognize how you value your money and how to use that valuation to your financial advantage.

Money fungibility may sound like the name of a mold spore growing on currency, but it's actually a term meaning that money is capable of being substituted for other money. Any U.S. $20 bank note is interchangeable with any other $20 bank note—or with two $10 bank notes, or four $5s, or twenty $1s, and so on.

The fact that money is fungible is the reason why I can lend you $10 and not expect to get the exact same bill back when you repay me. If I were to lend you my car, on the other hand, I'd be pretty steamed if you brought me back another one, even if it happened to be the same make and model. This is what makes money fungible and Honda Accords infungible.

The fungibility of money is important because all of the money in your possession is interchangeable. You might have money specifically set aside for an upcoming vacation, but you can certainly use it to pay a medical bill if you get sick before you have a chance to go on your holiday. Since money is fungible, it can be used for any purpose, not just the one you intend.

The problem is our brains have trouble remembering that money is fungible. We tend to assign different meanings and values to particular amounts of money, which leads to some truly bizarre financial behavior. This quirk of assigning meanings to different amounts of money is known as mental accounting.

What Is Mental Accounting?

Economist Richard Thaler was the first person to name the concept of mental accounting. He used the term to mean that we value money in different ways depending on where it comes from, what we plan to spend it on, and where we keep it. For instance, cash you receive as a gift for your birthday feels like "free" money for you to spend on something fun, even though you might make better use of it by paying your credit card bill. Our mental accounting draws a delineation between "real" money, which can be used for boring purposes like the Visa bill, and "free" money, which can be used for fun purchases.

Gambling wins are a very obvious place where we use mental accounting to ignore the fungibility of money. For many people, the money you win at a blackjack table or in a slot machine doesn't count as "real" money because it's not something you had to work to earn. This is why, for example, a person could bring $100 to Las Vegas to gamble, get up to $10,000 in winnings, and then lose it all in a single hand—and head home feeling as though he has only lost $100 total.

Of course, mental accounting is not just about gambling. You make financial decisions based upon your mental accounting on a daily basis since you keep running tabs in your head of various financial accounts. To test this, Thaler came up with the quintessential test of small-stakes mental accounting: "Imagine that you have decided to see a movie and have paid the admission price of $10 per ticket. As you enter the theater, you discover that you have lost the ticket. The seat was not marked, and the ticket cannot be recovered. Would you pay $10 for another ticket?"

What Happens in Vegas … Is Mental Accounting

The first (and only) time I went to Las Vegas, I discovered that gambling is not for me. I was in Sin City for a cousin's wedding, and my generous parents were bankrolling my minimal gambling. The first day, they gave my sister and me $50 each to spend on the slot machines, and I sidled up to an electronic poker game, full of excitement.

My first few rounds won me about $100, which spurred me to keep playing. Less than twenty minutes later, after seeing my winnings balloon to $200, I then lost everything. I stared at the machine in horror. All that money was suddenly gone. My sister comforted me by remarking that at least I hadn't lost any *real* money.

Her comforting statement—which ignored the fact that my father's $50 was just as spendable as $50 from my own bank account, to say nothing of the $200 I'd lost—is a common example of mental accounting. Gambling winnings and financial gifts don't feel like real money, according to the logic of mental accounting.

Most people would answer no to this conundrum. According to Thaler's research, only 46 percent of the people surveyed would purchase a replacement ticket after losing the first one. Change a single factor, however, and the answer is different: "Imagine that you have decided to see a movie where admission is $10 per ticket. As you enter the theater, you discover that you have lost a $10 bill. Would you still pay $10 for a ticket to the movie?"

Oddly enough, most people answer yes to the second question. According to the research, 88 percent of people surveyed would be willing to buy a ticket after losing a $10 bill. If you look at these two questions rationally, it's clear that you're out $20 either way. However, in the second scenario, the $10 bill you lost was not already earmarked for your movie. Your mental accounting of that lost $10 bill leads you to subtract the cost from some other fund in your mind, making the movie still only cost $10, rather than the harder-to-accept $20. Even though you are still out twenty bucks for the evening, you feel better about it when it is a $10 bill that got lost, rather than a $10 movie ticket.

Money may be fungible, but each dollar in your possession is not equivalent in your mind.

TAX REFUNDS: SEEING MENTAL ACCOUNTING IN ACTION

Tax season offers a unique opportunity to watch mental accounting on a national scale. Specifically, it's revealing to see how the majority of taxpayers use their tax refunds; this is a fascinating look at mental accounting.

People often plan to spend their tax refund on indulgences such as vacations, electronics, and the like. The average tax refund in 2016 was a hefty $3,120, which helps explain why so many taxpayers use their refunds for big purchases. When else would you have more than three grand burning a hole in your pocket?

The problem is that taxpayers are treating that $3,120 (more or less, considering that's an average amount) as if it is different from their salary. Even though your refund feels like a nice chunk of found money, it's actually your salary, which you have loaned to Uncle Sam interest-free. Theoretically, you could have saved up for your indulgence with the amount of taxes unnecessarily taken out of your paycheck each week, and earned a little interest from your savings account, to boot.

According to Shankar Vedantam, writing for *The Washington Post*, "Mental accounting influences how people deal with sudden gains, such as lottery winnings [or income tax refunds] . . . In terms of mental accounting, lottery winnings and refunds are invariably counted in the category of 'free money'—which is why people spend such dough not on healthcare, utilities, and eliminating credit card debt but on discretionary items such as vacations or new patios."

Compare this attitude with how workers plan to use raises. Knowing that you have an extra $2,000 coming this year because of a generous raise generally means you will start planning extra contributions to retirement, debt payoff, charity, or other (mostly) responsible ways to spend the extra money.

But if you get a $2,000 refund check come April 15, your view of the same amount of money changes, despite the fact that the moolah comes from the same source—your salary. When the money comes in the form of a tax refund, your mental accounting allows you to think of it as yours to blow, rather than money you need to spend responsibly.

The primary problem with mental accounting is the same one you might encounter with traditional accounting—forgetting the fungibility of money. For example, consider this traditional accounting error: Your boss tells you that you're free to take an unnecessary business trip since there's plenty of money in the travel account, but that you cannot buy an essential laptop because the equipment budget is empty. Arguing that you must have a new computer may fall on deaf ears, because the accounting at your workplace does not recognize the fungibility of budgeted money.

With mental accounting, you are similarly placing costs in separate categories in your head. For instance, let's say you budget $2,000 for a vacation. You and your family enjoy your time away, and make sure that you spend not a penny more than your budget on lodging, dining, activities, and souvenirs. Relaxed and happy, you come home . . . only to realize that there's not a scrap of food in the house and you owe your kennel $250 for taking care of Fido while you were away.

In this case, you have forgotten to account for the add-on expenses of your vacation because they do not fit into your mental vacation account. Fido's kennel costs and your empty refrigerator do not "count" as vacation costs in your head, so you neglected to budget for them with your mental vacation account. Your vacation budget should be closer to $2,300 because you need to buy convenience foods and pay for Fido's stay at the kennel as soon as you get home. But even after making this mistake one year, you are likely to fall victim to it the next and the next because it is very difficult to change your mental accounts of vacation expenditures.

Types of Mental Accounting Errors

Unfortunately, forgetting the fungibility of money is not the only way that mental accounting can lead you to mismanage your finances. Other types of mental accounting errors—specifically the denomination effect and the money illusion—can also lead to counterproductive financial behaviors.

THE DENOMINATION EFFECT

People are less likely to spend big bills compared to small ones. This phenomenon is called the denomination effect, a term coined by economists Priya Raghubir and Joydeep Srivastava in a 2009 research paper. If you have ever held on to a $50 or $100 bill for several weeks but don't blink an eye at spending the same amount in tens, fives, and singles, then you have experienced the denomination effect.

You might argue that the reason people hold on to large bills is because it is so inconvenient to break them. Just think of all the gas stations and convenience stores that post signs declaring that they will not accept $50 or $100 bills. But the denomination effect is not exclusive to big bills.

In an experiment conducted by Raghubir and Srivastava, eighty-nine college students were given $1, nominally as a thank you for their participation in an experiment. Half of these students were given a dollar bill, while the other half were given four quarters. The students were then told they could keep the money or purchase candy with it. The students proved more likely to spend their newfound riches if they received four quarters—63 percent of the participants receiving coins spent money on candy, whereas only 26 percent of the participants who received a dollar bill purchased any candy.

What's going on here? Why does it hurt so much more to spend a bill as compared to change? Ultimately you still have the same amount of money in your possession, but it *feels* different. There is an almost visceral pain at the thought of breaking a bill, particularly a large one, whereas coins or small bills can feel almost like "free money."

According to the researchers Drazen Prelec and George Loewenstein, that pain you feel when you break a bill is the effect of what they call coupling. This describes how much an experience of consuming something is tied to the experience of paying for it. For example, if you paid cash to enjoy a few margaritas with a friend, the act of enjoying your drink and the act of paying for it are directly coupled. The pain of paying is felt at about the same time as the pleasure of the tequila. (If you were to pay for your evening out with a credit card, the pain of payment is kicked down the road—an issue we will cover in more depth in Chapter 5.)

When you are paying with large-denomination bills, the pain of payment becomes larger, because your experience of the product or service you are purchasing is coupled with the loss of a physical symbol of a large sum. It's much harder to focus on the pleasure or utility you will receive from the purchase when you are focused on the loss of a large-denomination bill.

When Prelec and Loewenstein say that spending cash is painful, it's not an exaggeration. They teamed up with Brian Knutson, Scott Rick, and G. Elliott Wimmer for a neuroimaging experiment to determine what goes on in our brains when we make purchases. In the study, participants' brains were scanned by an fMRI while they made decisions about whether or not to purchase various products. The researchers found that when participants saw a product that was priced too high, the insula—the part of the brain that is associated with pain perception—had a corresponding increase of neural activity. So yes, it really *does* hurt to pay for a cup of coffee with a Benjamin.

THE MONEY ILLUSION

The term "the money illusion" was popularized by the famous economist John Maynard Keynes. It describes our inability to recognize that a dollar amount is only as good as its purchasing power. Keynes used the term to describe the phenomenon of feeling richer when you receive a cost-of-living raise, even though costs have also risen. In other words, you are earning the same purchasing power you did before the raise, but it feels as if you're earning more.

The money illusion also leads to mental accounting errors wherein you overspend because you are so focused on a high dollar amount in your possession. For instance, imagine you have just received a $3,000 bonus at work. You're feeling flush, so you may find yourself spending with impunity in every area of your life, from the expensive chocolate you rarely indulge in to new shoes that you don't really need. After all, you have an extra $3,000 in the bank, so you can afford to indulge. However, unless you are keeping careful track of each expenditure (which is the opposite of "spending with impunity"), you will likely reach the end of your bonus amount and keep on spending because you are focused on the large dollar amount you have received rather than what it buys. Your mental accounting of your bonus money has trouble keeping up with your actual spending.

Even if you are a The Price Is Right aficionado and know exactly how much your $3,000 will buy, it can still be easy to fall victim to the money illusion. Your enthusiasm about the large windfall can cause you to forget that your buying power is smaller than your excitement.

Children commonly fall victim to the money illusion since they are still learning the value of money. My mother loves to tell the story of how she was so excited about earning $25 when she was about twelve (in the early 1960s) that she decided to use it to take her entire extended family out for a lobster dinner. (Twenty-five dollars bought a lot more back then, but it still could not come close to paying for lobster for a family of five, plus assorted aunts and uncles.)

Most people have their own stories of childhood money illusions, and it is the sort of thing we believe that adults grow out of. After all, adults know better than to believe that they can pay for a lavish dinner with a little babysitting money.

However, for many people, the money illusion grows with them into adulthood. For example, a dear friend once told me about how she called her bank in a panic because she was sure someone had stolen $2,000 out of her checking account. She had been in a rigorous academic program and stopped paying close attention to her finances for about a month—until one day when she discovered her account had $2,000 less than she expected. After carefully reviewing all of the charges, she realized that she herself had spent the money. A month of $45 purchases here and there, dinners out, a gourmet coffee every day, and occasional runs to the ATM for cash all added up. In effect, my friend had stolen $2,000 from herself. No single expenditure was larger than $45 at a time, so her mental accounting had not caught up to her actual spending. She had mistakenly believed that $2,000 worth of purchases would "look bigger" because it was a large amount to spend.

Dealing with Your Mental Accounting

Though this chapter has dealt with the ways that mental accounting can lead you to make poor financial decisions, it's important to remember that mental accounting is essential for your daily transactions. The alternative to mental accounting is to consciously ask yourself what every purchase you make is worth to you, or worse, to cart around full accounting software to determine what each financial decision will do to your overall finances. Ain't nobody got time for that.

As weird and arbitrary as your mental accounting may be, you can mentally account for money in ways that help you improve your finances and ease your financial stress.

GIVE EVERY DOLLAR A HOME

One way to fight against mental accounting errors is to embrace the idea of mental accounting itself. Generally your mental accounting is unconscious. Making your accounting more mindful and deliberate will help you to avoid overspending. In particular, it's a good idea to give every dollar a home—that is, have a specific purpose in mind for all the money you earn.

There are two methods for doing this, and it's possible to do either or both at the same time, depending on what will work best for you:

Cash Envelope Budgeting

Debt-payoff guru Dave Ramsey has long touted the cash envelope budgeting system as an excellent method for controlling spending. This system makes your mental accounts completely tangible so that you are unable to overspend in any category. To set up the cash envelope system, determine what budget items you can consistently pay cash for, and then figure out how much money you should set aside in each category. Once you've done that, create an envelope for each one. For instance, you might create the following cash envelope categories:

- Car Repair
- Cleaning Supplies
- Clothing

- Charity
- Dining Out
- Entertainment
- Fun Money
- Gifts
- Groceries
- Haircuts
- Home Repair/Improvement
- Medical Expenses
- Office/School Supplies
- Pet Expenses

Once you have set up these envelopes, you will put the predetermined amount of cash in each one every payday, and only spend money from the envelopes for each category. This system makes it impossible for you to overspend any of your accounts unintentionally. If a friend invites you out to dinner and your dining out envelope is empty, you will know that you either have to borrow money from another account or turn him down. There is no way to fool yourself into thinking you are not overspending your dining out account because your accounts are tangible.

With the envelope system, it is also much easier for you to see when your mental accounting is faulty. For instance, the original movie ticket question, wherein your decision to buy a second ticket depends on whether you lost a ticket or a $10 bill, is much clearer if you are carrying a cash envelope. The $10 you lost in the second scenario would have come from your entertainment budget (since that's presumably the only cash envelope you'd be carrying), so you would have to acknowledge that you're paying $20 for the film no matter what.

Targeted Savings Accounts

Like cash envelope budgeting, targeted savings accounts allow you to allocate your money to specific budget categories or goals.

Instead of (or in addition to) setting money aside into various cash envelopes, you will open separate savings accounts for each of your budget/savings categories and set up automatic transfers to the various accounts on your payday. You might create the following targeted savings accounts:

- Car Repair/Replacement
- Education
- Emergency
- Furniture Repair/Replacement
- House Down Payment
- Taxes
- Vacation

Having such targeted savings accounts can help to ensure you do not accidentally spend your car repair budget on your vacation.

Many online banks offer customers the option of opening multiple savings accounts, and you often have the option to name each account based upon your savings goal. Capital One 360, Ally Bank, and SmartyPig are three online banks that allow customers to open multiple savings accounts under a single umbrella.

Creating either an envelope system or a targeted savings system (or both) will give your brain a break from the majority of your mental accounting. You will no longer have to carry your accounts in your head, since your envelopes or targeted savings accounts will have the information you need. This can make it easier for you to make more rational decisions with your money.

CARRY CASH—SPECIFICALLY LARGE BILLS

Personal finance experts have long recommended that people trying to tame their finances should switch to a cash-only lifestyle. As we discussed previously, paying in cash will always keep the pain of payment immediate in your mind, particularly if you have to break a large bill in order to make a purchase.

There are several potential downsides to this advice, however. First is that we are increasingly living in a cashless society, and not everyone is able or willing to switch to a cash-only life.

In addition, once you have decided to break a large bill, you may fall victim to the "what-the-hell" effect. This effect describes the loss of self-control after you have given in to a little temptation. For instance, once you have already decided to break that $100 bill in order to buy something, you might think, "What the hell! I might as well spend it all since it's no longer a nice crisp $100 bill anyway."

Finally, carrying cash can cause more mental accounting errors for individuals who are wired to see all cash as "free to spend" money. If this describes your brand of mental accounting, then carrying cash would be counterproductive.

RECORD ALL OF YOUR PURCHASES

There is an excellent reason why every financial book that shares shelf space with this book recommends that you track your expenses. Writing down every single penny that you spend can be an eye-opening experience. Not only will it help you find the leaks in your budget, but it can also help to disrupt any errors in your mental accounting. Since you must take the time to write down the ninety-nine cents for a new song on iTunes here and the $4.78 for a gourmet coffee there, you will have a much better understanding of how your various budget accounts are being spent.

Additionally, many times you might find yourself thinking you really don't want to write down a purchase. If seeing the reality of what you are about to spend in black-and-white does not appeal to you, then you probably don't really want to spend the money and would be happier keeping it in your wallet.

If tracking your expenses sounds about as entertaining as unmedicated dental work, don't worry. In Chapter 11 we will discuss methods for tracking expenses (and other important budgeting chores) with your psychology and preferences in mind.

KNOW YOUR OWN MENTAL ACCOUNTING ERRORS

The denomination effect and the money illusion can be seen as opposite ends of the same faulty mental accounting spectrum. The denomination effect means that it is very difficult to keep track of small amounts of money, whereas the money illusion can lead to over-spending due to an overabundance of enthusiasm for the high dollar amount.

Some people have trouble being financially responsible at both ends of the spectrum. They throw pennies away *and* overspend large amounts. Others are able to keep track of small amounts of money but fall victim to the money illusion any time they experience a windfall. Still others can make responsible decisions with large sums but let small amounts of money flow through their fingers because of the denomination effect. The savviest of money managers figure out how to be responsible on both ends.

Although it can be difficult to fight your nature, if you recognize that your mental accounting errors tend to fall at one end of the spectrum or the other, then it's okay to lean into your nature. For instance, you will never hear me giving blanket advice that all taxpayers ought to aim for a modest tax refund, even though a large refund represents an interest-free loan to the government. That's because any taxpayers who struggle to keep track of smaller amounts of money but feel comfortable making good decisions with a large sum will be better served with a check for three grand once a year as compared to an extra $60 per week that can be frittered away. For such individuals, the big tax refund is using the denomination effect to their advantage. Alternatively, those who have a tendency to burn quickly through windfalls would be in a better position to aim for a modest tax return and set up a direct deposit of the saved money into an investment, retirement, or savings account. That way, they can make the intelligent decisions about their money before they are faced with an amount that will trigger the money illusion.

Your mental accounting errors will often be consistent, so you might as well work with them rather than try to fit yourself into a system that doesn't work for you.

Chapter Three Takeaways

1. Money is fungible, which means it is interchangeable. Every dollar in your possession can buy just as much as any other dollar in your possession.

2. Mental accounting is a behavioral quirk that leads us to value money differently depending upon where it came from, how we plan to spend it, and where we keep it.

3. Mental accounting is essential for making decisions, but it can cause you to forget the fungibility of money and make counterproductive financial choices.

4. The denomination effect is a common mental accounting error wherein you are less likely to spend larger-denomination bills as compared to the same amount of money in smaller bills/change.

5. The money illusion is another common mental accounting error wherein you become so focused on the dollar amount of a large sum that you overestimate its buying power.

6. Common personal finance advice, including envelope budgeting, targeted savings, carrying cash, and tracking expenses, will all help to align your mental accounting with your actual financial situation.

7. Understanding the nature of your mental accounting errors can help you to work within your own behavioral quirks, rather than try to fight them.

PART TWO

Economic Reasons Why We Struggle with Money

Your money problems may feel unique, but many people struggle with the same financial issues you do, and for the same reasons. According to several theories of behavioral economics, a great deal of irrational financial behavior is common and predictable. This section will introduce you to economic behaviors that may be leading you astray and explain why we are all so susceptible to such mistakes.

CHAPTER FOUR

How Scarcity Affects Your Decisions

WHAT YOU'LL LEARN IN THIS CHAPTER

- Scarcity is more than just the phenomenon of having more needs than resources. It can also become a mindset.
- Living with the scarcity mindset can sharpen your focus on whatever you lack, but it will also tax your focus in other areas of your life.
- The scarcity mindset can also sap impulse control and motivation, making it more difficult for you to provide yourself with the resources you need.
- Though difficult, it is possible to outwit the scarcity mindset.

My eldest son was a terrible sleeper for the first eighteen months of his life. I dealt with his sleeplessness (and my own) relatively well in the first few weeks after he was born. I was coming into new parenthood well rested, and my husband and I had plenty of family visiting to help us out.

By the time our son was six months old, however, I was deep into a sleep deficit. I found myself resenting my husband's business trips (which often included sixteen-hour work days) because he got an entire night of silence through which he could sleep. It got to the point where we would sometimes have circular arguments about who got more rest on any given day.

I knew that sleep training would eventually pay off in better rest for all three of us, but I could not find the motivation to commit to any of the strategies I read about because it seemed like so much more work than I could handle. In my sleep-deprived state, I could barely take care of the little things that would help me feel more rested, such as changing into pajamas each evening. Committing to a sleep-training regimen was not even on my radar. I often found that I slept in my clothes or on the floor next to the crib rather than taking the time to get comfortably into bed. Of course, such sleep was hardly restful, making me even more tired the following day.

I can now say that I completely understand why sleep deprivation is prohibited by the Geneva Conventions—though I want to make it clear that my child had nothing in common with a war criminal. I was a barely functioning zombie for several of the most sleepless months of my son's infancy.

You might be wondering what this has to do financial stress. In a word: scarcity.

Scarcity is the phenomenon of having more needs than resources available to meet them. In my case, my need for rest was greater than the number of restful hours available to me. For those who are experiencing financial stress, their financial needs are greater than the amount of money available to meet those needs.

Scarcity is the issue behind both the cycle of sleep deprivation I experienced in early parenthood and the overwhelming cycle of financial stress many people experience daily. Trying to allocate scarce resources in a way that ensures we achieve all of our needs can cause great stress.

Scarcity is about more than just the lack of a needed resource. According to economist Sendhil Mullainathan and behavioral scientist Eldar Shafir, authors of the book *Scarcity: The New Science of Having Less and How It Defines Our Lives*, scarcity is also a mindset:

> Scarcity captures the mind. . . . when we experience scarcity of any kind, we become absorbed by it. The mind orients

automatically, powerfully, toward unfulfilled needs. For the hungry, that need is food. . . . For the cash-strapped it might be this month's rent payment. . . . Scarcity is more than just the displeasure of having very little. It changes how we think. It imposes itself on our minds.

Mullainathan and Shafir's research on the psychology and science of scarcity has made it clear that a great deal of the stress you feel about your cash flow is in your head—but that does not make it any easier to deal with.

How Scarcity Captures Your Mind

In researching their book, Mullainathan and Shafir came across a fascinating study from World War II that attempted to answer the question of how to go about feeding the millions of starving refugees who were being liberated by the Allies. Though the Americans and the British had enough food available to feed all of the hungry people they encountered, they did not know how to best reintroduce food to people who had been on the edge of starvation for so long. To answer this question, a team at the University of Minnesota conducted an experiment: Thirty-six healthy men volunteered to be put on a near-starvation diet and monitored.

The authors of the World War II study intended to determine the best method for feeding starving people, which they did—but they also unintentionally discovered the effects of scarcity on the mind. The starving volunteers began developing obsessions with cookbooks and restaurant menus. Some spent hours comparing produce prices in newspapers, while others daydreamed about new careers as restaurant owners. One volunteer said movie love scenes were not at all interesting to watch, while scenes featuring food were riveting.

These thirty-six volunteers had other compelling interests in their lives, but their lack of food pushed all other considerations aside. Their attention was overtaken by thoughts of food, even though not thinking about food probably would have made the ordeal easier.

Mullainathan and Shafir refer to this kind of intense and involuntary focus as "tunneling."

TUNNELING

The ability to focus when you are experiencing scarcity can be a good thing. For instance, even though I have a tendency to check my e-mail and social media multiple times a day when I am working, facing a tight deadline means I am able to ignore both the alerts that remind me I have received a new message and my own random impulses to see what is new on Facebook since the last time I checked it. This kind of focus is the reason why so many students are unable to work on essays or other schoolwork until the night before the assignments are due. The feeling of time scarcity brought on by a looming deadline can improve your focus so that you are able to be more productive with your work time.

Unfortunately, there is a dark side to that kind of focus. Once your focus becomes tunnel focus, you can easily forget anything outside of the tunnel that may need your attention. For instance, it is great when I can effortlessly ignore my social media, but it would be another matter entirely if I were to become so focused on my writing that I forgot to pick up my son from school.

Tunneling is a common reason why people get trapped in payday loan cycles. When you are facing an immediate money crisis—your car has broken down, for example, and you don't have the money to fix it—it is very easy to ignore the financial concerns outside of the immediate crisis, such as the rent payment that will be due in two weeks. So you take a payday loan to pay for your car repair. By the time you receive your paycheck and are in a position to pay back the payday loan, your rent is due, and you can't pay it without extending your payday loan. You solve that immediate crisis with an extension, but the fact that you will need to pay your utility bills the following week is not a consideration in the decision. Next week's bills are outside of the tunnel—and so the problem compounds.

Tunneling and Suicide

Tunnel focus can have devastating consequences, as a study published in 1978 proved. The study, titled "Where Are They Now?" followed up with 515 would-be suicides who were prevented from jumping from the Golden Gate Bridge in San Francisco between 1937 and 1971. The study found that 94 percent of the survivors were either still alive or had died from natural causes in the time since they were prevented from committing suicide. Dr. Richard Seiden, the study's author, stated that "suicidal behavior is crisis-oriented and acute in nature." In other words, individuals contemplating suicide are often tunneling on whatever problem they feel that suicide will solve. Individuals who have survived a jump from the Golden Gate Bridge describe a midair sensation of clarity about their tunnel vision. Ken Baldwin recalled to the *New Yorker* magazine that after he vaulted over the railing of the bridge, "I instantly realized that everything in my life that I'd thought was unfixable was totally fixable—except for having just jumped."

THE BANDWIDTH TAX

If tunnel focus were the only issue with the mindset of scarcity, it could be (somewhat) easily dealt with. On days that I have a tight deadline, I would know that I need to set an alarm to remind me to pick up my kid from school. Cash-strapped individuals tempted by payday loans could set similar calendar reminders to keep their upcoming bills on the top of their mind so that they could not ignore the potential costs of taking a quick loan. Even the terrible problem of suicide could be ameliorated with the installation of suicide barriers on places like the Golden Gate Bridge.

As a matter of fact, all those things do help to improve the scarcity mindset. Later in this chapter we will talk more about strategies for keeping your mind from ignoring issues outside of the tunnel.

However, Mullainathan and Shafir found that tunneling is only one of the ways that scarcity plays havoc on our brains. A more pernicious issue with scarcity is how it taxes your bandwidth—your capacity to focus your time and attention on any particular issue.

Though the word "bandwidth" may sound like the kind of business jargon that obscures meaning rather than describing anything, it's a very useful term when looking at how the human brain operates. According to Mullainathan and Shafir, "Bandwidth measures our computational capacity, our ability to pay attention, to make good decisions, to stick with our plans, and to resist temptations. Bandwidth correlates with everything from intelligence and SAT performance to impulse control and success on diets."

The problem with bandwidth is that it can be taxed when something else captures your attention. It is obvious when this happens due to an outside force. Trying to work in an office next to busy train tracks can be maddeningly difficult—as can trying to get work done when your child has come into the office with you. Your attention cannot help but be captured by the periodic rattling of a large locomotive outside your window or by the sound of your five-year-old saying, "Oops!"

But attention grabbers are not always external. Think back to the last time you had a big fight with a family member or were dealing with some sort of crisis. How much work were you able to get done? You may have been in a quiet office, but your attention was probably drawn over and over again to the argument or the crisis. Just like noisy environments, disruptive thoughts can tax your ability to pay attention.

Again, such internal disruptions would simply be an annoying fact of life if they were as occasional as your worrisome family arguments. Life happens, and people can have trouble concentrating after one-time disruptive events in their lives. You can expect to be distracted after a parent falls ill or your spouse asks for a divorce.

Financial scarcity is not generally a one-time event, though, and it has long-lasting consequences on your bandwidth.

The Difference Between $150 and $1,500

Mullainathan and Shafir decided to test their bandwidth theory with a simple experiment. They presented a random group of volunteers at a New Jersey shopping mall with one of two dilemmas. In the first, the volunteers were asked to imagine that they had car trouble which would require a $150 repair. The respondents were asked to decide whether they would fix the car now or wait a little while in the hopes that the car could last a bit longer without the repair. The second group of volunteers was asked the same question, with one difference: The car repair was now $1,500.

In both cases, volunteers were then asked to perform a series of IQ tests that measure fluid intelligence. Both groups were asked to report their annual income. Poor and rich volunteers did equally well with the IQ tests after considering the $150 repair question. But after considering the $1,500 repair question, poorer respondents had lower fluid intelligence scores. In fact, they lost as much as thirteen to fourteen IQ points simply by considering the possibility of a $1,500 car repair. To put that in perspective, a thirteen to fourteen point IQ difference is similar to the difference between your cognitive abilities after a good night's rest and your abilities after an all-nighter.

Mullainathan and Shafir argue that this erosion of cognitive performance is due to the bandwidth tax. If you struggle with money, just thinking about a financial burden means that your mental bandwidth is taken up with involuntary attention paid to your finances. The more well-off respondents did not deal with this kind of brain drain because the answer to the question about how to meet the challenge of a $1,500 car repair bill was relatively easy. They knew they could pay for the repair out of savings (or on credit), and their brains were free to then move on to the next problem. The poorer respondents had their brains stuck on the financial question since it was more difficult for them, and they therefore had less bandwidth available for the IQ test.

What's worrisome about this finding is that being preoccupied by financial concerns makes you measurably less intelligent than you would otherwise be and thus less able to deal rationally with those concerns.

Impulse Control and Motivation

A common assumption about individuals stuck in cycles of poverty is that they are personally responsible for their situation. It is understandable why this assumption is so widespread. Not only does our society tend to assign moral meanings to poverty (as we discussed in Chapter 1), but it can be very easy for outside observers to see ways that the impoverished wrestle with impulse control and motivation. The struggling individual who succumbs to temptation and purchases something unnecessary—whether it is as cheap as a latte or as expensive as an iPhone—seems to lack the moral fortitude necessary for impulse control. The impoverished single parent who drops out of the night classes that could lead to a better paying and more stable career seems to lack motivation to better her situation.

However, considering all we have learned about scarcity in this chapter, it should be clear by now that there is more going on than lack of personal responsibility. Scarcity affects our ability to make decisions, and tunneling and the bandwidth tax in particular work to derail both impulse control and motivation, creating a feedback loop of scarcity. Once your focus and bandwidth are compromised by scarcity, then you have fewer mental resources available when you need to exert self-control.

For instance, imagine you have been dieting all week, subsisting on preplanned meals of salad and lean protein even when your coworkers head out of the office for lunches at local eateries. The mere process of dieting has given you a scarcity mindset, wherein your focus is tunneled on all the treats you are denying yourself; likewise, your bandwidth has been taxed by thoughts of calorie counts. Now imagine that you arrive home from work on Friday to find a flyer on your door advertising two-for-one deals from a pizza joint down the street. On a normal week, you could probably throw the flyer away without giving it a second thought. When you are coming off a week of dieting, however, how easy will it be for you to ignore the temptation of pizza for dinner?

Living in poverty offers a similar situation—except instead of the food temptations a dieter must resist, the poor must resist spending money, even on things they may need. As Mullainathan and Shafir put it, "When you can afford so little, so many more things need to be resisted, and your self-control ends up being run down."

The supposed lack of motivation exhibited by the impoverished can similarly be attributed to the scarcity mindset. Education is often seen as the antidote to poverty, but antipoverty programs that rely on education and training see a great deal of absenteeism and drop-outs. While it is easy to point to the impoverished themselves as the problem—after all, if they were really motivated to better their situation, the argument goes, nothing would keep them from such classes—Mullainathan and Shafir argue that the bandwidth tax is the more likely culprit. If you are overwhelmed by financial concerns, it may be difficult to pay attention in class, and you might quickly feel at sea with the material. Similarly, if you are depleted by your scarcity mindset, it may seem much easier to miss a class after a rough day, since the benefit from the class is far in the future, whereas a quiet night at home will help today. Once you've missed one class, the next one is that much more difficult to understand, and dropping out starts to make more sense than trying to catch up.

Combatting the Scarcity Mindset

The scarcity mindset is an almost universal phenomenon. Whether you are dealing with financial scarcity, or time, sleep, or caloric scarcity, your brain will react to the experience of scarcity in a predictable manner. Just because we can determine what our brains look like on scarcity does not make dealing with the scarcity mindset any simpler. However, there are several practical methods for combatting the effects of scarcity on your brain:

BUILD SLACK INTO YOUR BUDGET

The difference between the lower-income and higher-income volunteers in Mullainathan and Shafir's IQ test experiment was that the higher-income volunteers had some slack in their budget to handle a

$1,500 car repair. If you know there is money available to you to handle one of life's unexpected emergencies, then you are less likely to fall victim to tunneling or the bandwidth tax. This is why every personal finance expert on the planet tells people to begin their financial journey with an emergency fund.

Of course, it's very easy to say, "Build some slack into your budget." Actually doing so can feel nearly impossible when you are already dealing with financial stress. Here are some ways to create financial slack even when you think you have none:

Automatically Transfer $10 per Week to Savings

Saving money will always be the last thing on your mind when you have bills to pay, so take it completely off your mind through automation. A regular transfer of a small amount of money to your savings account allows the money to move without your attention or focus on it. Choosing a small dollar amount may seem counterproductive—after all, what will $10 per week do? However, choosing an amount of money that you know you will not miss helps you to gradually grow your savings account. In addition, the small amount will make it not worth your while to transfer it back, unless and until you need to access the money for an emergency.

Increase Your Automatic Transfer Amount in the Future

Of course, $10 per week only adds up to $520 per year, which is hardly the kind of slack that will ease the bandwidth tax. So it's important to use your tunnel focus on the present to your advantage by setting up automatic increases of your savings transfer at regular intervals. It's very easy to plan to increase your $10 per week to $25 per week three months from now, since you are not focused on the issues you'll be facing in the future. Taking the future decision out of your hands allows you to increase your savings rate without affecting your bandwidth.

Decide Now How You Would Quickly Raise Money

In 2011, the National Bureau of Economic Research published a paper that examined Americans' ability to handle financial emergencies. According to the paper, approximately one-quarter of Americans report that they would be unable to come up with $2,000 within thirty days, and an additional 19 percent would only be able to come up with such cash by pawning or selling possessions, or through taking out payday loans.

Living with that kind of financial fragility will affect your mindset, so it pays to be proactive. You may not know how you would generate $2,000 or $5,000 or $10,000 in an emergency, but you can take some time to think through methods for coming up with that kind of cash *before* such an emergency strikes. That way, you can give thought to the problem when your brain is not also overburdened by the emergency itself.

What strategies might you consider? Pawning or selling some items could help, as could borrowing from a friend or family member. Take the time to plan out a course of action for how you can generate money in an emergency so that all you have to do when the emergency strikes (if you have not yet built up the emergency fund to take care of it) is put your plan in action.

BREAK INTO YOUR TUNNEL FOCUS

When you are tunneling due to the scarcity mindset, you often end up ignoring other issues that can cause you even more trouble down the line. Here are two ways you can plan ahead for the inevitability of tunnel focus.

- *Set reminders.* It took me many years to realize that the people who appear to be born organized are not any more mindful or better at juggling than the average person. No, those born organized are simply better at setting reminders for themselves. For instance, if you have a report for work that you absolutely cannot forget the next morning, placing your keys on top of the report will remind you to take it when you are tunneling on the importance of getting to work on time. When it comes to combatting financial scarcity, setting up automatic bill-pay reminders can do a great deal to help you keep future finances on the top of your mind. Similarly, many banks also offer e-mail alerts to remind you when funds get below a certain point or when drafts over a certain size are taken from your account. These small reminders can help you bring outside issues into your tunnel.

- *Send your future self a letter.* The site futureme (www.futureme.org) allows you to draft and send an e-mail to yourself in the future. A strategic use of such a service can allow you to remind yourself to pay irregular bills, increase savings, sign up for a retirement account, and the like. You will not have to rely on your own faulty memory within the tunnel to get these things done.

Chapter Four Takeaways

1. Physical scarcity is the phenomenon of having more needs than resources.

2. Living with scarcity "captures your mind" and changes the way your brain works. This is the scarcity mindset.

3. A scarcity mindset causes intense focus on whatever it is that you lack. This can be beneficial in the short term, but it can also cause tunnel focus, which means you overlook anything outside of the tunnel.

4. Bandwidth is your ability to pay attention and make good decisions. The scarcity mindset taxes your bandwidth, to the tune of thirteen to fourteen IQ points.

5. Living with a scarcity mindset also weakens your impulse control and your motivation. From the outside, this can make poverty look like a moral failing, but the behaviors are attributable to the bandwidth tax.

6. Building financial slack into your budget—through strategic savings and careful thought about how you would raise money in an emergency—can help to combat the bandwidth tax of financial scarcity.

7. Setting reminders for yourself can help you to keep important issues from being neglected when you are tunneling.

CHAPTER FIVE

The Cognitive Biases Causing Your Financial Stress

WHAT YOU'LL LEARN IN THIS CHAPTER

- A cognitive bias is a systematic error in logical thinking.
- Such biases are common and even predictable, but it can be very difficult to detect cognitive biases in your own thought patterns.
- Seven of the most common cognitive biases are likely behind some of the counterproductive and stress-inducing financial behavior you engage in.

One of the astonishing things about the human brain is its ability to make quick decisions based upon huge amounts of random data. We do this in part through the use of what are called heuristics—mental shortcuts that allow us to make fast and efficient judgments. Without these mental shortcuts, we would be bogged down by all the calculations necessary to make decisions.

For example, let's say you've picked out some clothes at a store: a pair of jeans priced at $39.98, a shirt priced at $29.97, and a scarf priced at $19.95. You have about $100 in cash—$95, to be exact. How would you determine if you have enough money to cover your purchase?

While the most precise method of answering that question would involve adding the exact amounts together, it's much more likely that you would round up each price and add the approximations. It takes a heck of a lot less time to do this than it would for you whip out paper and pencil or a calculator, and the approximation will give you a useful answer. The heuristic of rounding prices helps you to determine that the $100 or so in your wallet will cover the approximate $90 cost of your new clothes.

Heuristics smooth out difficult decision-making processes, meaning you do not have to overload your brain with information and calculations every time you need to make a decision. The problem with heuristics is that they can sometimes result in a cognitive bias.

Cognitive biases are systematic errors in logical thinking that can lead to poor decisions. We are all vulnerable to cognitive biases because the heuristics we use to approximate answers are more like rules of thumb rather than absolute truths. But our brains have trouble recognizing when such a rule of thumb is leading us astray.

For instance, let's go back to the clothing store. The total of your purchases equals approximately $90 ($89.90, to be exact). You know you have about $100 in your wallet, so you stride up to the register, prepared to pay. But the rounding heuristic did not take into account the 7 percent sales tax on your purchase, or the fact that you are thinking of the $95 in your wallet as "about" $100. So when the total comes to $96.19, you feel foolish when you realize you are more than a dollar short of the total purchase price. The rounding heuristic gave you an informal sense of how much you would owe at the register, but it became a cognitive bias when you failed to recognize that the amount you calculated was not exact.

Cognitive biases affect every part of our lives, from our work habits to our political beliefs, and they can be very difficult to recognize. Unfortunately, cognitive biases can often lead to irrational money behavior that adds to your financial stress.

Though researchers have identified dozens of cognitive biases (and have theorized, but not necessarily proven, even more), the following seven biases are among the ones most likely to negatively affect your financial behavior:

Anchoring

Anchoring is a heuristic that helps you to determine a fair price for something without having to do exhaustive research. The anchor is a price point that gives you an idea of how much something should cost.

For example, suppose you go out for a nice meal with your family. You want to order a bottle of wine for the table, but not knowing much about wine, you're not certain what you should purchase. You see that the wine list includes a $70 bottle of wine, so seeing the $30 bottle listed next to it seems like an incredible steal.

You have to ask yourself if that is really the case. You probably would have been just as happy with a $15 bottle, but since you came into the situation without a clear idea of how much to spend, you're likely to fall victim to the anchor price of $70 and purchase the $30 bottle. In fact, restaurants understand this effect very well and will often only keep one bottle of the expensive wine on the premises. It's only there to sell the "mid-priced" wine, since no one's really going to order it. The anchoring heuristic is being used against you in this case, because you don't have a good sense of what a decent bottle of wine should cost.

It is very difficult to ignore anchor prices. Once you have a set price of something in mind, it can be tough to remember that the anchor you've been using might not have anything to do with a rational price you want to spend.

What is even more troubling about anchoring is that our brains don't need a number to be an actual price to change our behavior. Focusing on any random number prior to a financial opportunity will influence the amount you are willing to pay. Dan Ariely, the behavioral economist and author of *Predictably Irrational* whom we met in Chapter 2, proved this with a fascinating experiment. Ariely and his research partners asked a group of fifty-five college students to jot down the last two digits of their Social Security numbers and then state whether they would pay that amount in dollars for a number of different products. These included bottles of fine wine, a box of gourmet chocolates, and several cordless computer products. From there, the researchers asked the students to bid on the products in an auction.

Ariely found that "the students with the highest-ending Social Security digits (from 80 to 99) bid highest, while those with the lowest-ending numbers (01 to 20) bid lowest." The last two digits of the students' Social Security numbers should have had zero effect on the amount they were willing to pay for the various products that were offered, but our brains are so wired to hold on to an anchor number that we will latch on to an unrelated number if that's all that is available.

COMBATTING THE EFFECTS OF ANCHORING

One way to circumvent the problem of anchoring is to create your own anchor to redefine the amount of money you would otherwise spend. A friend of mine did this when she was a poor college student and she thought of everything in packages of ramen (her go-to cheap meal, which cost only $0.25 each) rather than dollars. If she wanted a new CD, $14 might seem reasonable, but fifty-six ramens (nearly two months of dinners!) was far more than she could afford to spend. This type of thinking also made it possible for her to avoid the temptations of the bargain section, since a $5 album was still worth twenty meals to her—and she needed the food more than she needed the tunes.

That strategy worked well for a poor college student, but for anyone past the ramen stage of life, converting dollars into time might be a more effective strategy. This suggestion comes from the book *Your Money or Your Life* by Vicki Robin and Joe Dominguez. In the book, the authors point out that we all trade our time away in order to earn money, so anything we buy using money actually costs us time. Since time is gone once it is spent, looking at prices of goods in terms of hours worked is a better indicator of cost than dollars.

To translate dollars into time, you need to figure out how much you earn per hour, and then calculate how much things cost in terms of hours worked. For instance, let's say you make $20 per hour. You have your eye on a new laptop that costs $1,500. But if you change the price from $1,500 to seventy-five hours, does the laptop still seem like a good buy? Just remembering how much of your life you would have to give up for a purchase can help you to spend only on the things that reflect your goals or improve your life.

Ultimately, changing your anchors into a currency that you are more able to think about rationally—whether that currency is time or ramen—allows you to better understand what things really cost.

The Availability Heuristic

The availability heuristic is a kind of memory shortcut that helps you determine how likely something is. Your brain assumes that things you can easily recall are more probable than things that are hazier.

Let's try a little experiment.

Make a list of all the words you can think of that begin with the letter R.

....

Now, come up with a list of all the words you can think of that have R as the third letter in the word.

....

Based on your lists, which is more common: words beginning with R or words with R as the third letter?

If you said words beginning with R, you've just fallen victim to the availability heuristic. It's much easier to come up with a list of words beginning with R, so our brains believe that R words must be more common—but it's just not true. Our brains have assigned more probability to the idea that initial-R words are more common, because it was so much easier to come up with a list of initial-R words.

That ease of recall helps explain many common phobias. For instance, people are often very scared of air travel, despite its overwhelming safety, because every plane crash makes national and international news. However, those same phobics drive cars daily even though, statistically, driving a car is a much more dangerous mode of travel. It's easier to imagine a plane crash because we learn about every single one of them from the news, while the 100-plus car fatalities that occur every day receive scant coverage.

Similarly, modern parents tend to be frightened of the possibility of their children being kidnapped, though there has literally never been a safer time to be a child. Statistics on crime rates don't matter to worried parents who can call up the names and images of children who have been abducted. The fact that we can remember those kids means we overestimate the probability of something similar happening to our own children.

The Gambler's Fallacy

The gambler's fallacy is a phenomenon related to the availability heuristic, wherein you believe that something must happen because it's "due" to occur. For example, if you toss a coin fifteen times and it comes up heads each time, you might feel pretty confident in betting that the sixteenth toss will come up tails. What are the odds that a coin will come up heads sixteen times in a row, after all? But this thinking ignores the fact that each individual toss has $^{50}\!/_{50}$ odds, no matter what happened before. The previous tosses have no effect on the future.

Investors "playing" the stock market can make similar mistakes. For example, some investors will buy into stocks that are in a fifty-two-week low on the theory that they are "due" to go up. Others might avoid buying stock that's currently on fire, fearing that the good times can't possibly last. In both of those cases, there is more going on. You truly are gambling with your money if you believe that everything evens out every time.

To combat the gambler's fallacy, you need to look at your stock choices (and coin tosses) rationally. Each independent event has its own odds—regardless of what your brain argues.

Such misalignment of probabilities based on recall is a big enough problem. It is made worse by the way our memories work. Emotional memories tend to be recalled more strongly than neutral ones, meaning anything we can remember to which we had an emotional reaction will seem more likely to happen to us.

When it comes to finance, the emotional aspect of memory means we don't have a store of memories of individuals retiring comfortably after being diligent savers and savvy investors, even though that is a fairly common occurrence. You have no doubt heard your share of stories about such individuals, though you may not recall them clearly. Instead, we remember lottery winners, investors who became wealthy overnight, and big-winning gamblers. Those stories are exciting, even if they are relatively rare, and so our memories latch on to them. Being able to recall a local lottery winner makes it that much easier for you to imagine what it would be like for you to win, and your brain then assumes that the scenario is not only possible, but probable. Each time big winners are featured on news and human-interest stories, it becomes even easier for our brains to think the big payout could happen to us.

COMBATTING THE AVAILABILITY HEURISTIC

Anecdotes are the currency of the availability heuristic. Every time you hear of a lottery winner, a 100-year old smoker, or a kidnapped child, you are adding to your brain's store of available outcomes, whether or not those outcomes are truly likely. Since those outcomes appeal to our emotions, they will stick in our minds.

So how do you combat this heuristic?

You need to recognize when there is an emotional component to your decision. Does your choice reflect any kind of statistical probability, or does it simply *feel* as though the outcome you are hoping for (or alternatively, trying to avoid) is the likeliest one?

It is also helpful to spend time educating yourself on financial statistics (or alternatively, accident fatality or crime statistics, depending on where your availability heuristic leads you astray) to help you understand when your reaction is irrational.

Hedonic Adaptation

Hedonic adaptation describes the phenomenon wherein we get used to the things we have. Think of the pleasure and pride you felt upon first purchasing your car. I'm guessing your delight in your new vehicle faded before the new car smell had completely dissipated. This happens because our brains are wired to get used to things fairly quickly.

This can be both good and bad. In 1978, researchers from Northwestern University and the University of Massachusetts asked recent lottery winners and recent paraplegic victims of catastrophic accidents about their levels of happiness. As you might expect, the lottery winners were happier than the accident victims immediately after their life-changing events. However, both groups returned to their average level of happiness within two months. They got used to their new normal, which meant they were about as happy as they were before their lives changed.

For most of us, hedonic adaptation is not the result of a major life change. It merely means that no purchase or consumer good will permanently satisfy us. Unless we truly examine the reasons why we are making purchases, we are likely to keep reaching for another thing to buy that will offer momentary pleasure. However, each new thing will quickly become old hat, prompting another purchase.

Hedonic adaptation is why it is so easy for a major pay raise or other financial increase to land you in the same financial stress you felt at a lower level. When the purchases that were rare treats when you were poorer become a standard part of your life, you enjoy them less. The upshot is that you will be loath to part with them now to improve your financial life, because they are part of your new normal. This is why behavioral economists have started referring to hedonic adaptation as the hedonic treadmill—you have to keep running faster and faster just to stay in the same place enjoyment-wise.

COMBATTING HEDONIC ADAPTATION

Researchers studying the science of happiness have found that there are two ways to control the sense of hedonic adaptation. The first is through gratitude. Regularly expressing gratitude for the things in your life can help you feel both more optimistic and happier, according to Robert A. Emmons, professor of psychology at the University of California, Davis. That increased happiness can help end the constant search for pleasure through purchasing, which is what the hedonic treadmill represents. According to Emmons, a gratitude journal, wherein you regularly record things for which you are grateful, can help you improve your mood, as well as your physical and social well-being.

In addition, spending your money on small and regular pleasures will provide you with greater satisfaction than you would feel by saving all of the money up for a larger indulgence. Hedonic adaptation means you will soon become accustomed to the new car or the week at the beach. However, having a standing movie date with your best friend every Saturday will be something that you get to enjoy over and over, and look forward to throughout each week. Hedonic adaptation will not have a chance to rob you of your pleasure in enjoying your favorite films with your favorite person.

Hyperbolic Discounting

Imagine I were to offer you $50 right now—or you could wait two weeks and I'll give you $55. If you're like most people, you would choose the instant money, even though waiting a mere two weeks would give you 10 percent more—a rate you'd kill for from any investment.

That preference for instant gratification is human nature. It's also the reason why we have so much trouble saving for retirement, losing weight, and quitting unhealthy habits. Our brains are wired to prefer the instant, the immediate, and the now over the future. Behavioral economists call this hyperbolic discounting.

What's happening here is that you "discount" things that will happen in the future as being less important than those things occurring right now. For instance, you might be planning to fit back into your size 8 dress for your class reunion in April, but the moment the waiter comes by with the dessert tray, your virtuous plans go out the window. April is so far away, and chocolate cake is in front of you right now.

We all fall victim to these sorts of decisions that we later come to regret. In a lot of cases, we know that we will regret those decisions while we are making them. Sadly, our impulse to discount the future is so strong that we chow down on the cake while thinking, "I'm going to hate myself for this in April!"

In essence, we are borrowing from our future selves by pushing today's consequences into the future. We decide that avoiding the consequence today means that the consequence is not our problem, even though it will be when the time comes. Credit card companies build their businesses on you borrowing from your future self. Maybe you are like many other people who find it very difficult to save up money now to buy something later. With a credit card, it's easy for you to fall for the instant gratification now and convince yourself that later can take care of itself.

HYPERBOLIC DISCOUNTING AND THE PAIN OF PAYMENT

In Chapter 3, we discussed that spending cash (and particularly spending large bills) hurts more than paying with a credit card. That sensation is known as the pain of payment, and hyperbolic discounting is a major contributing factor to how credit card spending decouples your purchase from the pain of payment. You place the consequences of paying for your purchase upon your future self, and in so doing you pay attention only to the pleasures of your purchase in the here and now.

According to a study by Promothesh Chatterjee, assistant professor of marketing at the University of Kansas School of Business, consumers using credit cards pay more attention to the benefits of the product they are buying, ignoring the costs. Because the pain of purchasing the product has been decoupled from its benefits, consumers are more likely to weigh those benefits in a vacuum, without considering the price.

For example, suppose you have $50 in cash to spend on a lovely meal out with your spouse. While the surf and turf sounds delicious, you don't want to be embarrassed when the check comes and your fifty doesn't cover the meal, let alone the tip. So you order from the right side of the menu and end up with a safely inexpensive pasta dish.

If, on the other hand, your plan is to pay for dinner with credit, then you have much less reason to worry about how much the lobster costs per pound. That means you're more likely to think about how mouth-watering any particular dish may be as opposed to how much it will set you back. A check arriving for double what you planned to spend can be shrugged off if you can pay for it easily with credit.

COMBATTING HYPERBOLIC DISCOUNTING

One thing to remember is that the hyperbolic discount ceases to have an effect when you place the decision past a certain time threshold. In the previous hypothetical example, where you could choose $50 now or $55 in a couple of weeks, would your decision be any different if I asked you whether you'd like $50 on February 4 of next year or $55 on Valentine's Day? In this case most people will happily wait. Since you are waiting until next February for the money anyway, it is easier to decide to wait the additional ten days for the extra 10 percent.

The effect of hyperbolic discounting diminishes as you place decisions in the future, which offers you a method for combatting the effect. Imagine your current dilemma as if it will happen in the future. Doing this can help you to see the issue more rationally and help you come to the decision that your future self will be glad you made. Similarly, making choices with your future self's happiness in mind (which we will cover in depth in Chapter 12) can also help you to remember that instant gratification is not actually gratifying.

Illusory Superiority (a.k.a. the Lake Wobegon Effect)

If you've ever listened to Garrison Keillor's NPR show *A Prairie Home Companion*, you'll remember that its fictional location, Lake Wobegon, is the place where "all the women are strong, all the men are good-looking, and all the children are above-average."

This tag line explains why the cognitive bias originally called illusory superiority is often referred to as the "Lake Wobegon Effect." Every one of us has a tendency to perceive him- or herself as above average, which is obviously mathematically impossible. Several experiments have borne out this cognitive bias, including a 1981 study that found 93 percent of the American drivers surveyed believed they were above average in driving skills, and 88 percent believed they were above average in terms of driving safety.

The Lake Wobegon Effect can be a huge problem for investors. Believing that you are a better investor than average can lead to attempts to time the market—that is, buy stock at its lowest and sell it at its highest. As we will discuss in Chapter 6, you have to be correct about timing the market 82 percent of the time in order to simply match the returns you will likely get if you buy and hold your investments over a period of decades.

If you need any proof that investors are vulnerable to the Lake Wobegon Effect, look no further than the difference between how the market has done over the past twenty years as compared to how average investors have fared. Between 1993 and 2013, the stock market as a whole has seen an 8.21 percent return per year on average, despite two recessions—but the average investor has only gotten 4.25 percent return per year over that time. Since the average investor has reacted irrationally to market volatility, rather than buying-and-holding his investments, he has missed out on growth.

COMBATTING ILLUSORY SUPERIORITY

David Dunning, a former psychology professor from Cornell University, has, along with his colleague Justin Kruger, studied illusory superiority. According to Dunning there are a few ways to mitigate the errors you are likely to make due to your sense of illusory superiority:

Learn More about the Subject

Since you don't know what you don't know, avoiding your sense of illusory superiority is incredibly difficult. This is why it is always a good idea to educate yourself on any issue that will require you to make a decision with long-lasting consequences.

Seek the Opinions of Well-Informed and Trustworthy People

An expert can help you figure out where you might be going astray or where there are potential problems that have not occurred to you.

Take Your Time

People are more likely to fall victim to illusory superiority if they are making a quick or impulsive decision. Deliberating prior to making your decision can help you to minimize any errors. This is because taking some time to think through the issues might reveal errors or problems that would not immediately occur to you, a non-expert. In particular, Dunning suggests that explicitly considering ways in which you might be wrong or missing something about a decision can help you to determine if you are making the right choice. For instance, you might ask yourself what could be wrong with a car being sold at a great price, or why no one else has jumped on the no-fail Bolivian tin mine investment opportunity.

Restraint Bias

How strong do you think you would be in the face of temptation? Most people believe they are perfectly capable of ignoring temptations—but then they find themselves falling off the wagon as soon as their control is tested. This common cognitive bias is known as the restraint bias, and it's related to illusory superiority.

The Hot-Cold Empathy Gap

Researchers have found that our restraint bias is often triggered by something known as the hot-cold empathy gap. This gap is a cognitive bias that leads you to underestimate how much your visceral needs (like hunger or lust) and/or your state of mind (like anger or frustration) will influence your behavior. For instance, if I were to ask you right after dinner if you will have any trouble bypassing the office donuts the following morning, you will probably answer that you won't. When I ask the question, you are full and satisfied from dinner, which means you are imagining yourself the next morning feeling the same way. By the time morning comes, however, you may be hungry or tired, which will make you much more likely to grab a chocolate glazed donut than you could have anticipated when you were full and alert.

Most people tend to overestimate their own impulse control. They believe they will be able to show more restraint in the face of temptation than is realistic. This is why your grand plans to lose twenty pounds are often derailed by the first box of donuts you see. You have overestimated your ability to be virtuous in the face of temptation.

The restraint bias is often the culprit when you find you cannot maintain the resolution (or budget, or schedule) you have set for yourself. When you are in the midst of planning the new resolution, budget, or schedule, you are certain that you'll be able to restrain yourself around your temptations and that you'll be perfectly capable of handling all of the issues that may come up under your new rules. Unfortunately, you will be just as flawed and human in the future as you have been in the past—but the restraint bias will keep you from remembering that fact.

COMBATTING THE RESTRAINT BIAS

In the Greek epic *The Odyssey*, Odysseus longs to hear the dangerous song of the sirens, who use their enchanting voices to lure sailors to their deaths. Odysseus plugs his crew's ears with beeswax and has them tie him tightly to the mast of his ship. This allows him to hear the sirens' song without having the ability to steer the ship off course.

Odysseus's example shows us how to combat the restraint bias. If you know ahead of time that you will be tempted, set up your life so that you cannot make the poor decision once temptation strikes. We will talk in Chapter 12 about ways to do this.

The more pernicious issue with the restraint bias occurs when you don't know that you will be tempted. Though unexpected temptations will always crop up, you can help mitigate both the restraint bias in general and the hot-cold empathy gap in particular by keeping a daily journal while you work to improve your finances. In each entry, jot down how you felt when you made decisions, particularly the decisions you are most or least happy with. Over time, you will begin to see the emotional and thought patterns that repeat as you make your best and worst decisions. Once you know when you are most tempted and what is most likely to lead you into temptation, you will be in a better position to avoid those situations.

The Spotlight Effect

In 2000, researchers at Cornell University asked fifteen undergraduate students to don a T-shirt featuring a photograph of the singer Barry Manilow (whose coolness quotient had definitely dipped since the release of "Mandy") before going into a room full of strangers. The Cornell researchers then asked the Manilow-wearing participants to estimate how many of the strangers in the room recognized Barry's smiling face. The participants, feeling embarrassed by the T-shirt, predicted that about half of the other students in the room would identify the face on their shirt as belonging to Manilow. In reality, less than 25 percent of the strangers in the room recognized who was on the shirt (and I'm assuming they were all humming "Copacabana" to themselves).

What's going on here is something called the spotlight effect. This is the cognitive bias that leads you to believe that people are noticing you more than they really are. Wearing a T-shirt emblazoned with Barry Manilow can be so embarrassing to the wearer that it seems impossible to believe other people won't notice it. However, other people *don't* notice—because they are too busy feeling mortified about the pimple on their chin or the hole in their shoe.

The spotlight effect can have a big effect on spending if you worry that other people will notice your spending habits. For instance, many young professionals believe they must own a nice car in order to do well in their careers. That belief is based upon the idea that their superiors, coworkers, or clients are judging them by what car they drive.

Unless you have a job such as a real estate agent, which involves clients getting into your car, it's likely that no one even knows what kind of vehicle you drive. Even if you do work as a real estate agent, people are much more likely to notice that your car is clean and well kept than recognize how new or expensive it is.

A similar problem occurs when people find they need to downsize in some way. If you are worried about what people will think if you move to a smaller home or let your membership to the club lapse, it can be very easy for you to maintain unnecessary and unsustainable spending just to keep up appearances.

COMBATTING THE SPOTLIGHT EFFECT

We all believe we are the hero of our own movie, which makes it difficult to remember that other people are not paying as close attention to us as we believe. The best way to combat this effect is to adopt something sociologist Martha Beck calls the universal question: So?

Asking yourself "So?" is useful because it both helps you to remember that people are not paying as close attention as you think they are, and it helps you to put the issue in context. Does whatever you are embarrassed about really matter?

Here is how you might use Beck's universal question:

"Everyone will see that I bought a ten-year-old used car."

So?

"If we downsize, people will think we couldn't afford our mortgage."

So?

This thought exercise can help you to recontextualize the financial decisions you make based on embarrassment or shame, since it helps you remember that no one is paying attention and nothing bad will happen if you change your habits.

Chapter Five Takeaways

1. Our brains are wired to use mental shortcuts (known as heuristics) in order to quickly make decisions without being bogged down by information. When these mental shortcuts lead us astray, they are called cognitive biases.

2. Anchoring is the phenomenon wherein the first price you hear for a product or service becomes the standard by which you measure other prices.

3. The availability heuristic leads you to believe that something you can easily recall is likely to happen.

4. Hedonic adaptation describes how you become accustomed to any changes in your life so that you no longer notice the benefits that once gave you pleasure.

5. Hyperbolic discounting refers to our preference for instant gratification over future benefits.

6. Illusory superiority is the cognitive bias that causes us to assume we are better than average.

7. Restraint bias describes our tendency to overestimate our ability to resist temptation in the future.

8. Because of the spotlight effect, we all tend to believe that others are paying more attention to us than they really are.

CHAPTER SIX

Our Fear of Loss

WHAT YOU'LL LEARN IN THIS CHAPTER

- Loss aversion is a cognitive bias that causes us to feel losses far more strongly than we feel gains.
- There are natural mistakes that all humans make due to the effects of loss aversion.
- Precommitment mechanisms can help you avoid loss-averse behavior.

Imagine you have just stepped into Caesars Palace in Las Vegas to make a $50 bet—which you promptly lose. Now, you have two choices in front of you. Accept the loss and stop gambling or attempt to win back your lost fifty-spot. Are you going to turn around and leave, $50 poorer, or will you make another bet in order to try to recoup the lost money?

If you're like most people, you'll probably decide to try to win your money back, since the chance you *might* win back your lost cash is enough of a motivation for you to overlook the reality that the house typically wins in the end.

According to Shankar Vedantam of NPR, the second bet is actually an easier gamble for you to make than the first one was:

People seem much more willing to place the second bet than to place the first bet. And that's because with the first bet you're hoping to win something. With the second bet what you're really trying to do is . . . head off the loss.

What's going on here is a cognitive bias known as loss aversion, wherein your brain is hardwired to avoid pain ahead of seeking pleasure. The psychological pain you feel from losing $50 is about twice as powerful as the pleasure you would have gained from winning the same amount of money. Since pain is a strong motivator for human beings, we tend to work hard to avoid those painful losses—harder than we would work to achieve gains. Unfortunately, loss aversion often leads to behavior that is counterproductive.

Nick Leeson and the Downfall of Barings Bank

The British financial institution Barings Bank was founded in 1762 and enjoyed a global reach, but it only took one man's loss aversion to destroy it. Nick Leeson was hired as a trader by Barings in 1989 and quickly earned a reputation for his expertise and nearly infallible decision-making abilities. His profits alone constituted nearly 10 percent of Barings' total profits in 1993, so the bank's higher-ups felt little need to supervise his aggressive trading.

When one of Leeson's employees suffered a small £20,000 (approximately $38,000) loss on his watch in July 1992, he worried about losing either his reputation or his job. Leeson hid the loss in an error account and tried to make the money back through speculative trading in which he was not authorized to engage. His speculative trades led to more losses, which he continued to hide, until the losses represented millions and millions of pounds. The ultimate downfall came in January 1995 when a desperate Leeson bet on the Nikkei Index in Japan, just as a major earthquake in the Japanese city of Kobe sent the index into a downward spiral. The bank's ultimate losses totaled £827 million ($1.4 billion) as of February 26, 1995, and Barings collapsed literally overnight. ING bought the institution for £1, and Nick Leeson went to jail. His attempt to avoid losing his reputation over a small amount of money led to a chain of events that caused him and his employer to lose everything.

Let's go back to the casino. You lost the $50 and decided to try to win it back. But you lose the second bet, as well, meaning you are now out $100. Naturally, this loss feels even lousier than the initial loss. The rational thing to do is quit playing before you lose any more money. It may hurt to leave the casino with your wallet noticeably lighter, but ending your night of gambling after two lost bets is objectively the smartest course of action for anyone who can't afford to lose any more money.

For many people, however, walking away no longer feels like a viable choice. For loss-averse individuals who are focused on their lost cash, just getting back to their starting point becomes something close to an obsession. If you feel as if you can't walk away from the money you've lost, how much more would you have to lose before you stopped playing? For some people, that answer is "everything."

Your Finances on Loss Aversion

Loss aversion rears its ugly head in more places than just the casino. You feel the effects of loss aversion in your everyday life. For instance:

- Have you ever held on to an investment longer than you should have?
- Are you reluctant to cancel the gym membership you never use?
- Do you have a bread machine (or a treadmill) in your basement that you've used only once or twice?
- Have you ever listed your house at a higher price than your real estate agent recommended?
- Are you willing to wait in line for the latest gadget (or hottest concert ticket) to make sure you don't miss out?

Every single one of these behaviors is an example of loss aversion— and all of them can cost you money and cause you unnecessary financial stress. Let's explore some of the ways that loss aversion can destroy your finances:

INVESTING AND LOSS AVERSION

As much as the financial industry might deny it, the psychology of investing in the stock market has a lot in common with the kind of gambling that goes on at a casino. In particular, the psychological pain you feel when you lose money in your stock portfolio is no different from the pain you feel when you lose money at the blackjack table. That pain triggers loss aversion, and it causes us to make the same mistakes in investing that we do when we gamble. Specifically, we overreact to both major losses and major surges.

For instance, the market crash of 2008 prompted many investors to sell their tanking investments. Their fearful reaction was a perfect example of loss aversion. Seeing the housing bubble burst made them fear that all their investments would soon be worth nothing, so they liquidated their investments—and possibly considered burying the cash in the backyard.

What loss-averse investors forgot was that the market tends to return around 10 percent *over time*. This means investors need to weather downturns and trust that the market will recover. Otherwise, getting out of the game after a loss means that you have made a temporary loss a permanent one.

According to Joni Clark, chief investment strategist for asset management firm Loring Ward, "everyone who converted to cash in 2008—especially after the market dropped—locked in those losses, which meant they also missed the market surges that took place in 2009. Investors who sold out of the equity market for the safety of cash in early March may have locked in losses of close to 25 percent for the year-to-date 2009, and may have missed out on a 58 percent stock market rebound (as measured by the S&P 500 Index)."

The other side of the loss-aversion investing coin is continuing to sit on investments that are going gangbusters in the hopes they will keep going up and up. Though this decision may feel like it is motivated by "irrational exuberance" rather than fear, it ultimately comes down to a fear of potential losses. If the stock you are holding is doubling in value every week, you will fear that getting out will leave money on the table that could have been yours if you'd had the nerve to hold on to the stock. You would hate to be the idiot who sold your gazingus pin stock for $12 per share when it ends up trading at $75 per share just a few weeks later.

Such surges are generally the result of loss aversion. Everyone is afraid of missing out, so the market inflates very quickly while investors pile onto the new trend. However, the inflating stock prices don't actually reflect the stocks' legitimate worth based upon the underlying company's prospects. Which means the bubble eventually bursts, the stock price drops, and all of the loss-averse investors then cash out, locking in their losses.

If one of your investments is going through the roof, it is always possible that you might be able to time the market and liquidate at the height of the surge. However, the greater likelihood is that waiting will only result in losses. It doesn't feel good to kick yourself for quitting when there was more money to be made, but it hurts far more to lose money because you sat on a rising investment until the price peaked, and then started falling.

LOSS AVERSION AND CLUTTER

All across the nation, there are panini presses, Bowflex machines, and ski equipment gathering dust in basements, attics, garages, and storage facilities. I have a set of adjustable weight dumbbells in my basement that cost $300 and have been used fewer than a dozen times.

Loss aversion explains why it is so difficult to get rid of this home clutter. Not only are we afraid that as soon as we get rid of such items we will need them (even though there has been no indication that we will become panini-making, weight-lifting skiers at any point in our lives), but we are also loath to part with something we spent "good money" on. We'll talk more about that second fear in the section on the endowment effect. For now, let's examine your fear that you'll need something the moment you get rid of it.

It can feel like there is no harm in keeping unused items around your house. You've got the things you might need right there, which means you're saving money by never having to rebuy something you have already owned once.

Unfortunately, that is not the case. Allowing your loss aversion to dictate what items you keep in your home is actually costing you money:

You Rebuy Items Anyway

If your home is cluttered with things you might need someday, that makes it much more difficult for you to locate any one item when you do need it. Often, that means you end up buying a second rake when you can't locate the first one because it was hiding behind the Bowflex.

You Waste Time

In 2004, Newsweek magazine reported that the average American spends fifty-five minutes per day looking for things she knows she owns. Nearly an hour per day of fruitless searching equals roughly two weeks' worth of your time each year—time you could be spending more productively.

Storage Costs

Whether your excess belongings are sitting in your basement or in a storage facility, it is costing you money to store them. Storage facilities are the more obvious cost, since the average price for a 10- × 20-foot unit is $100 per month. But holding on to items in your own home can also cost you, particularly if you live in a more expensive home than you can afford in order to keep all the stuff you are afraid to lose. Also, don't forget the money you might have to spend in order to safely store your items. For instance, anything stored in a basement needs to be in an airtight plastic container and presided over by a dehumidifier, unless you are prepared to chuck it all when the rainstorm hits that finally breaches your cellar.

LOSS AVERSION AND RECURRING CHARGES

Similar to our reluctance to divest ourselves of items we don't use, loss aversion also leads us to hold on to subscriptions or other recurring charges we don't use. For instance, according to the site Statistic Brain (www.statisticbrain.com), as of December 2015, 67 percent of gym members never use their memberships. They are allowing an average of $58 per month to be debited from their accounts and are receiving no benefit from it. This irrational money behavior comes from the fear of losing access to the gym. You still have the option to go if you keep the membership, but you completely lose that option if you cancel it—even though you know you're not going to go to the gym.

Marketers are well aware of this tendency, which is why you'll find that most gyms impose a hefty joiner's fee. Even if your fear of losing access to the gym doesn't keep you paying for your membership, the thought of having to pay the joiner's fee a second time can be enough to force you to maintain a membership you don't use. Never mind that you've probably wasted the equivalent of a second joiner's fee by the time you've let a couple of months go by without a visit to the gym.

LOSS AVERSION AND THE ENDOWMENT EFFECT

The mere fact that you own something can make you overvalue it. This is an aspect of loss aversion known as the endowment effect.

For instance, in a classic study by Daniel Kahneman, Jack Knetsch, and Richard Thaler, about half of the study participants were given mugs and then offered an opportunity to sell the newly acquired mug. Meanwhile the rest of the participants were presented with the same type of mugs and were asked how much they would be willing to pay to buy one. The mug-owning participants wanted twice as much money to sell their mugs as non-mug-owning participants were willing to pay to purchase a mug.

These were standard mugs, of the sort you can pick up at any store—but that didn't matter. Once the participants felt a sense of ownership over the mugs, they valued their mugs more highly.

This phenomenon is related to the reason why retail clothing stores often offer bags or baskets for gathering your potential purchases. Retailers know that once you have held an item in your hand, you're psychologically tied to it and don't want to give it up. The longer you have it in your possession, the stronger that connection, and the more you are unwilling to part with your new stuff.

The endowment effect is another reason why we tend to keep things we don't use. The fact that we spent "good money" on an exercise bike or small appliance blinds us to the item's actual value. We recall that we spent $400 on the item, and we hate to lose that amount of money. However, as we look at the item—covered in several years' worth of basement dust and smelling slightly moldy—it should be clear that its value is much lower now. The endowment effect makes us feel as though we cannot sell the item for anything less than what we paid for it, even though we ourselves would not pay that asking price for the item right now.

This is a common reason why selling a home can be so frustrating. For instance, when my husband and I relocated from Lafayette, Indiana, to Milwaukee, Wisconsin, we set too high an asking price for our Indiana home. It was next to impossible for us to look objectively at the home where we had lived for six years. Not only had we worked hard over the years to improve the house and make it our own, but it was also where we brought our two newborn sons home from the hospital. It was not just a house to us, so it was a struggle to price it realistically. Ultimately, we lowered our price several times and ended up accepting an offer that was only a few thousand dollars higher than the price we'd paid for the place in 2010—an amount that felt almost insulting. The endowment effect made it nearly impossible for us to just be glad that our home sold.

LOSS AVERSION AND FOMO

If you're new to the concept, FOMO stands for "fear of missing out." It is the form of loss aversion which kids these days are most likely to be affected by. (By the way, the inclusion of FOMO in a personal finance book means that the term will never again be used by anyone under the age of thirty-five. I apologize for the death knell of a useful term.)

FOMO is the social anxiety we feel when we worry about losing out on something better than what we are already doing or already have. Like the opportunity costs we discussed back in Chapter 2, FOMO is the insidious sensation that you have not maximized your opportunities.

The problem with FOMO is that you can easily forget what partaking in any fun activity will cost. For instance, when you are drooling over your friends' Instagrammed brunch photos while eating a bowl of Cheerios in your bathrobe, you tend to focus on how much fun they are having and how delicious the free-range gluten-free French toast looks, rather than the reality that they have probably blown $45 on brunch.

There are several different ways that FOMO can break a budget:

Experiences

This is the classic FOMO expense. You spend money going out with friends, rather than finding cheap or free ways to have fun together. Fear of missing out on experiences can be even more devastating to a budget if there is an income disparity among a group of friends. It's very easy to spend to keep up with your richest friend, rather than suggest cheaper alternatives or face the prospect of spending the evening with Netflix and leftovers.

The Latest Gadget

The folks who line up overnight in order to be the first to score an iPhone 3.1415s are not camping out because they are convinced that the slightly improved product is going to change their lives—rather, they are afraid of what they will miss out on if they do not upgrade.

Technology seems to change at light speed these days, and not only do we fear missing out on cool new features, but we also fear becoming the luddite who doesn't even know how to use the most popular apps.

Time

There is an incredible time cost to FOMO since those affected by it constantly check for updates. If you are doing this on your own time, it may not cost you money per se, but it can certainly harm your relationships.

But who hasn't also checked Facebook or Twitter at work—or when he should have been studying? Loss of productive time because you are afraid of missing something can be incredibly costly.

Precommitment Mechanisms Will Foil Your Loss Aversion

Loss aversion is so deeply written into our psyches that it is extremely difficult to change loss-averse behavior. Psychologists have found, however, that using precommitment mechanisms—methods of taking a future choice away from yourself—can help protect you from the effects of loss aversion. These mechanisms take choice out of your hands when you would otherwise be tempted to engage in loss-averse behavior.

There are several precommitment mechanisms you can use to combat the various types of loss aversion we've discussed in this chapter:

COMBATTING INVESTMENT LOSS AVERSION WITH A BUY-AND-HOLD STRATEGY

Back before GPS devices were invented, I used to regularly panic while driving to a new place if I stayed on the same road for too long—even if that was exactly what my directions told me to do. I had a tendency to worry that I was going the wrong way if I wasn't actively making turns or merging onto new roads. (You could say I was "getting-lost averse.")

That feeling of panic is a familiar one to many investors. It's common for us to feel as if we need to take an active part protecting our investments if things seem to be going poorly—even though we may know that statistically our money is in the best possible investments.

My Mother's Precommitment to Ocean City

When my mother was in her early twenties, she had a phobia about driving over bridges. She decided to conquer her fear by driving across the Chesapeake Bay Bridge-Tunnel, which spans 23 miles in total, 12 of which are the type of trestle bridge that made Mom nervous.

Rather than just jump in the car and go, Mom did two things to make sure she would return triumphant. First, she called and made a reservation at a posh hotel in Ocean City, Maryland. Then she called all of her friends to let them know she was spending the weekend at the beach. Both of those actions made her feel as though backing out of the drive was not an option. Losing her hotel deposit and losing face with her friends both felt worse than white-knuckling her way across the bridge—which meant her precommitment mechanisms worked perfectly.

What's going on here is called the "action bias," and it kicks in when there appears to be uncertainty or a problem. This cognitive bias means that in the face of an ambiguous situation wherein we may potentially suffer a loss, our universal preference is to do something—anything! According to researcher David Wilkinson on the blog *Ambiguity Advantage* (http://ambiguityadvantage.blogspot.com), "we are happier doing *anything*, even if it is counterproductive—rather than doing nothing, even if doing nothing is the best course of action." Our loss aversion triggers the action bias when our investments take a sudden dip, and it can feel like torture to sit on our hands if there might be *something* we could do. The action bias is one of the reasons why people sell when the market is at its lowest and buy when it's at its highest. They are afraid of doing nothing.

In point of fact, simply sitting tight on your investments is by far the smartest way to grow your money. According to research by Nobel laureate William Sharpe, you would have to be correct about timing the market (that is, buying stock at its lowest and selling it at its highest) 82 percent of the time in order to simply match the returns you will get if you buy-and-hold your investments over a period of decades. To put that in context, Warren Buffett aims for accurate market timing about two-thirds of the time.

Committing to a savvy, long-term, buy-and-hold strategy is the way to take loss aversion out of the equation when you invest. With such a strategy, you can ignore the action bias that your loss aversion triggers when there are market downturns. That's because you will know that you made the best decisions for your money ahead of time, before your emotions got involved. As long as you have chosen an investment strategy that fits your needs and timing, then you want to keep your hands off of it for the long haul (other than regular rebalancing, which I'll discuss in the next section).

COMBATTING INVESTMENT LOSS AVERSION WITH REBALANCING

In addition to the tendency to sell investments at a loss when things are going poorly, loss aversion also causes irrational investing behavior during market surges. That's when you avoid selling any of your rapidly rising investments for fear that they will continue to grow and grow without you. Alternatively, you may sell lower-performing investments in order to buy more stock in whatever is going gangbusters.

Any given stock or market sector can suffer huge losses (and likely will, if it is going through the roof all of a sudden), which is why every investing expert preaches the importance of diversifying your investments. However, diversifying your investments when you initially invest is not enough. It's also vital that you rebalance your investments on a regular basis.

For instance, if you originally allocate 60 percent of your portfolio to stocks and the market experiences an increase, you may find that stocks now represent 80 percent of the value of your portfolio. That means your portfolio is riskier than it was when you started, so it's a good idea to rebalance. There are three ways to do this:

1. Sell some investments from overweighted asset categories, and use the proceeds to make purchases in your underweighted asset categories. (An asset category is a group of investments that have similar characteristics. For instance, stocks might be one asset category in your portfolio, bonds might be a second, and money market accounts might be a third.)

2. Purchase new investments from the underweighted categories.

3. If you are still making regular and/or continuous contributions to your portfolio (as you are probably doing with your 401(k) or IRA), then you can change your contributions so that more of your investments are in the underweighted asset categories until your portfolio is rebalanced.

Regular rebalancing is an important part of keeping your portfolio healthy and in alignment with your investment goals. It is also something you should plan on doing no more frequently than every six to twelve months. More often than that, and you risk triggering the action bias. In addition, the fact that you are committed to regular rebalancing means you have set aside time to make decisions about buying and selling, which will make you less vulnerable to loss-averse investing behavior in between your regularly scheduled rebalancing.

COMBATTING CLUTTER WITH THE ONE-YEAR BOX

This rule is a great precommitment mechanism that will allow you to determine just how often you use things you are afraid to give up. Place all of the items you don't use but don't want to get rid of into a box, and date it for one year in the future. If you have not used the items in the box within that year, then donate or trash the box without opening it. It's likely you won't even recall its exact contents.

If the items you are holding on to are large enough that they won't fit into a box (such as that Bowflex), drape a sheet over them and place the date on the sheet. This will give you the same visual sensation of boxing them up—and it will make it easier to sell or donate the items after a year since you won't have to clean twelve months' worth of dust off of them.

COMBATTING RECURRING CHARGES WITH GOOGLE CALENDAR

As with physical clutter, you need to be reminded that you are not using subscriptions. Since you can't put your gym membership into a box, use Google Calendar (or any other digital calendar app you use) to set a reminder for one month in the future. Have the reminder ask you, "How many times have you been to the gym in the past month?" If the answer is zero, cancel your membership. If you have gone to the gym at least once, set another reminder for the following month. At that point, if you have not made gym-going a habit (at least one workout per week), cancel your membership. You can always purchase day passes or explore other workout opportunities to handle your occasional workouts.

COMBATTING THE ENDOWMENT EFFECT

There is not much we can do to combat the endowment effect once we already own an item, as any frustrated home seller can attest.

However, you can avoid triggering the endowment effect through pre-commitment mechanisms before you buy.

Don't Touch Anything at Stores

When you are out shopping, avoid picking up any items you don't want to buy. It's much easier to leave the cute purse or new gadget behind if you've never thought of it as "mine!"

Refuse Any Free Trials

When you're offered a free trial period for anything, such as HBO with your cable package, just say no if it's not something you're currently willing to pay for. The cable company knows you will be willing to pay more in three months to keep your fix going than you are to buy it outright. That's why they offer the trial.

COMBATTING FOMO

While there is no way to completely turn off your fear of missing out, there are several ways to use precommitment mechanisms to keep FOMO from breaking your budget.

Schedule Fun Ahead of Time

FOMO is most likely to strike if you find yourself on Friday afternoon staring down an empty weekend. Instead, schedule your fun ahead of time. Not only will you be less tempted by last-minute invitations, but you will also enjoy your planned outing even more than a spontaneous one. According to psychologists who study the science of happiness, we feel an extra boost of pleasure when we consciously delay enjoyment. Looking forward to your board game night or your weekend camping trip will add to the pleasure of those events—something even a last-minute invitation to a lavish party can't offer.

Take a Social Media Fast

The big surge in the feeling of FOMO is due to the rise of social media. Back when you heard about the awesome party after the fact or only learned of your old roommate's incredible vacation to Hawaii when you randomly ran into him at the store, there was no time for you to worry about missing out on other people's awesome experiences.

These days, we know about things in real time, and it can make us feel anything from envy to regret. According to a 2013 study entitled "Facebook Use Predicts Declines in Subjective Well-Being in Young Adults," the more people use Facebook, the worse they feel after logging off.

Turning off the social media—whether for a couple of hours, days, or weeks—can do wonders for making you feel better about your own life. For starters, you won't be able to compare your regular life to the polished version of your friends' lives online. In addition, we often check social media due to boredom, and taking a break from your feeds can prompt you to get back to the cool hobbies you don't have time for anymore. Nothing kills FOMO faster than working on something you enjoy.

Carry Cash

A simple way of fighting FOMO in the moment is to make sure you only carry cash on your nights out. The last-minute invitation to a swanky club sounds a lot less tempting if you either have to drink nothing but water or stop at the ATM on the way. Having even a moment to think about whether you really want to do something can be enough for your better nature to prevail.

Chapter Six Takeaways

1. The pain we feel at the prospect of a loss is twice as strong as the pleasure we feel at the prospect of a gain. For that reason, our brains urge us to avoid losses more than they urge us to seek gains, which is often counterproductive.

2. We are likely to engage in loss-averse behavior while gambling and investing, but loss aversion also affects our willingness to keep or discard items and memberships, as well as the way we spend our social time.

3. Precommitment mechanisms are methods of taking future choices away from yourself. Savvy use of precommitments can help you avoid most types of loss-averse behavior.

PART THREE

Psychological Reasons Why You Struggle with Money

Though your money problems are not unique, your reaction to money is both personal and idiosyncratic. In order to end your financial stress, you must dig into the psychological reactions you have to money in your life. This section will allow you to examine the role of money in your life and the stories you have told yourself about money since your childhood. The next three chapters will help you identify the psychological and personal obstacles that have kept you from achieving your financial goals and show you methods for correcting or working around those obstacles.

CHAPTER SEVEN

Money Scripts

WHAT YOU'LL LEARN IN THIS CHAPTER

- A money script is an unconscious core belief about money. Such scripts inform everything you do with money.
- Money scripts fall into four categories, although many people follow scripts from more than one category.
- Certain money script categories are associated with specific types of disordered financial behavior.
- You can and should personalize strategies for reducing your financial stress based upon your money scripts.
- Journaling can help you to literally edit your destructive money scripts.

As we discussed at the beginning of the book, you cannot separate your use of money from how you feel about money. No one is perfectly rational on the subject. But your irrational reaction to money is not necessarily like anyone else's irrational reaction. That's because your essential beliefs about money grew from the experiences in your life—specifically your experiences in childhood.

These money beliefs, which financial psychologist Dr. Bradley Klontz calls "money scripts," are the stories about money you have told yourself since your childhood. Money scripts are rooted in how money was viewed in your family home when you were growing up, and they are often reinforced by your life experiences with money.

Money scripts can be either helpful or harmful to your financial stress level. And they most certainly have a lasting effect on how you spend, save, and feel about money.

The Four Types of Money Scripts

According to Dr. Klontz and his research partner Dr. Sonya Britt, money scripts fall into one of four categories:

1. Money Avoidance

2. Money Worship

3. Money Status

4. Money Vigilance

MONEY AVOIDANCE

Individuals with money avoidance scripts believe either that money is bad or that they do not deserve money. Common thinking in this category runs along the lines of *Most rich people do not deserve their money* or *Good people should not care about money.* These scripts are based upon the idea that money is a source of anxiety, fear, or disgust—and that living with less money is a virtue.

MONEY WORSHIP

Money worship can be seen as the opposite of money avoidance. It's based on the idea that money can lead to happiness and fulfillment. If your scripts fall into this category, you may think things like *It is hard to be poor and happy* and *You can never be too rich.*

MONEY STATUS

If you are operating according to money status scripts, you conflate your net worth with your self-worth. You might think things like *Success is measured by how much money I make* or *My possessions reflect my importance and worth.*

MONEY VIGILANCE

If you think along the lines of money vigilance scripts, you probably think things like *Money should be saved, not spent* and *I have to research all purchases to make sure I get the best deal.* While these scripts can help your finances, if taken too far, they can have a negative effect on your psyche. For instance, following a money vigilance script can cause intense feelings of guilt when you spend money on yourself.

What Money Script Do You Follow?

Once you know which money scripts most affect your financial behavior, you'll be in a better position to combat any self-destructive or stress-inducing choices those money scripts prompt you to make. The short version of the Klontz Money Script Inventory (Worksheet 7-1), which appears courtesy of Dr. Bradley Klontz, can help you determine which money scripts most shape your beliefs about money.

OVERLAPPING SCRIPTS

While many individuals will generally fall into only one category of money script, it is possible to have several overlapping scripts from different categories.

For instance, avoidance and vigilance are two money script categories that seem to correlate well. Even if you are uncomfortable with owning money, it still makes sense to try to keep careful track of the money you have. Similarly, money worship and money status beliefs dovetail in obvious ways. Believing that more money will equal more happiness is related to the belief that your net worth is synonymous with your self-worth.

But Dr. Klontz often sees two money scripts that seem to be diametrically opposed:

"Sometimes we have a lot of correlation between people who are money avoidance and also are money worshipers. They may seem to be totally opposite approaches to money, but when you think about it more holistically, it does make sense. The people who are so adamantly against rich people—if you actually sit down with them, they actually would like to be rich."

Not only can having these conflicting beliefs be emotionally taxing, but it can also lead to some seriously poor financial decisions. You might financially sabotage yourself in order to avoid becoming wealthy—while still compulsively spending what money you do have in the hopes that it will help you to feel happier.

YOUR MONEY SCRIPT IS NOT "WRONG"

When I introduce the idea of money scripts to people in classes or seminars, a common misapprehension among my audience is that money vigilance is the "right" type of money script, while the other types of money scripts are "wrong." Since money vigilance often tends to help one's bottom line, it follows that people believe it's the "right" way to view money.

However, it's important to remember that your money scripts are neither right nor wrong—they are simply the financial lens through which you look at the world. In fact, all money scripts carry an element of truth to them. Dr. Klontz writes about this subject on his site Your Mental Wealth (www.yourmentalwealth.com):

Worksheet 7-1: What's Your Money Script?

Scoring Scale:
1 Strongly disagree 2 Disagree 3 Disagree a little 4 Agree a little 5 Agree 6 Strongly agree

MONEY AVOIDANCE	MONEY WORSHIP	MONEY STATUS	MONEY VIGILANCE
I do not deserve a lot of money when others have less than me.	More money will make you happier.	I will not buy something unless it is new (e.g., car, house).	It is important to save for a rainy day.
1 2 3 4 5 6	1 2 3 4 5 6	1 2 3 4 5 6	1 2 3 4 5 6
Rich people are greedy.	You can never have enough money.	Your self-worth equals your net worth.	You should always look for the best deal, even if it takes more time.
1 2 3 4 5 6	1 2 3 4 5 6	1 2 3 4 5 6	1 2 3 4 5 6
It is not okay to have more than you need.	Money would solve all my problems.	Poor people are lazy.	If you cannot pay cash for something, you should not buy it.
1 2 3 4 5 6	1 2 3 4 5 6	1 2 3 4 5 6	1 2 3 4 5 6
People get rich by taking advantage of others.	Money buys freedom.	If something is not considered the "best," it is not worth buying.	I would be a nervous wreck if I did not have an emergency fund.
1 2 3 4 5 6	1 2 3 4 5 6	1 2 3 4 5 6	1 2 3 4 5 6
Your score: _____	Your score: _____	Your score: _____	Your score: _____

If you scored a 9+ ... Money avoiders believe that money is bad or that they do not deserve it. They believe that wealthy people are greedy and corrupt and that there is virtue in living with less money. Avoiders may sabotage their financial success or give money away in an unconscious effort to have as little as possible. Money avoidance is associated with ignoring bank statements, increased risk of overspending, financial enabling, financial dependence, hoarding, and having trouble sticking to a budget.

If you scored a 9+ ...At their core, money worshipers are convinced that the key to happiness and the solution to all of their problems is to have more money. At the same time, they believe that one can never have enough. Money worshipers are more likely to have lower income, lower net worth, and credit card debt. They are more likely to spend compulsively, hoard possessions, and put work ahead of family. They may give money to others even though they can't afford it, or be financially dependent on others.

If you scored a 9+ ... Money status seekers see net worth and self-worth as synonymous. They pretend to have more money than they do and as a result are at risk of overspending. They believe that if they live a virtuous life, the universe will take care of their needs. They tend to grow up in families with lower socioeconomic status. People with money status beliefs are more likely to be compulsive spenders or gamblers, be dependent on others financially, and lie to their spouses about spending.

If you scored a 9+ ... The money vigilant are alert, watchful, and concerned about their financial welfare. They believe it is important to save and for people to work for their money and not be given handouts. They are less likely to buy on credit. They also have a tendency to be anxious and secretive about their financial status. While vigilance encourages saving and frugality, excessive wariness or anxiety could keep someone from enjoying the benefits and sense of security that money can provide.

Every money script has an element of truth in it. Not the whole truth, mind you, but an element of truth. For example, while the [non-money] script *Flying is dangerous* is partially true, it is not the whole truth. Other parts of the truth are missing, such as *Flying is safer than being a pedestrian in a major city*, *Flying is safer than riding a bicycle*, or *Flying is safer than traveling by car*. Money scripts work the same way. While they represent a part of the truth about money, they typically do not represent the whole picture. Operating as if they are the complete and absolute truth, without regard to context, can be disastrous.

Any money script can lead to disordered (and disastrous) financial behavior, including money vigilance scripts. Those with money vigilance scripts could find themselves becoming miserly and losing personal or professional relationships due to their devotion to saving money. Though this may not result in financial disaster, it does not make the loss of family or friends any less disastrous.

It's also important to note that money vigilance does not necessarily protect you from wasting money. For instance, a money vigilant individual I know attended an out-of-state undergraduate university because it was listed as a "best value" by *U.S. News & World Report*. Once he got to campus, he discovered that part of what made the school a "good value" was that it was a commuter school for the vast majority of the students. The campus emptied out on evenings and weekends, meaning he had trouble making friends and felt very isolated. He transferred to another school after one year, which cost him money and time that he would not have had to spend if he had not been following money vigilance scripts as a prospective student.

While vigilance scripts often tend to be helpful to those who carry them, they are no less likely than any other scripts to lead to disordered behavior that can cause you stress. In addition, there are aspects of avoidance, worship, and status scripts that can lead to more satisfying financial decisions even if those decisions do not necessarily aim to maximize the use of your money.

Ultimately, it is useful to examine your money scripts with an attitude of curiosity and discovery and let go of any notion of "right" or "wrong." That insulates you from any shame or guilt you might otherwise feel upon uncovering your money scripts.

How Your Scripts Are Stressing You Out

Though your money scripts are unique to you, there are some disordered financial behaviors that are common to the different categories of money scripts. Once you have identified the scripts you follow, you need to understand the ways in which those scripts leave you vulnerable.

MONEY AVOIDANCE PROBLEMS

The following are several of the common difficulties facing individuals with money avoidant scripts.

Financial Denial

Individuals who follow money avoidance scripts often retreat into financial denial in order to avoid money stress. This denial can take the form of anything from refusing to open bank statements and bills to letting a spouse or family member take care of all financial decisions. Avoiders who engage in financial denial may be congratulating themselves on the fact that they are "above" money concerns, since they believe that only shallow people care about money; they may believe that it is impossible for them to ever get ahead and so it is unnecessary to keep track of their finances; or they may believe that finances cannot or should not be any of their concern.

The first step to ending financial denial is a little like the first step to weight loss—you need to be willing to know how bad it has gotten by stepping on the scale. In the case of financial denial, the "stepping on the scale" moment means gathering up all of your financial information and looking through it carefully.

Squandering Wealth

If you feel that you do not deserve to have money, then suddenly receiving a windfall can be very stressful. I experienced this situation when my father passed away in 2013, leaving me as one of the beneficiaries of his life insurance policy. Though I don't generally feel that I am undeserving of money, one of my money scripts specifies that I don't deserve money I didn't earn. Add to that my feeling that it was disloyal to my father to experience any enjoyment of the insurance money, and it's no wonder I tied myself in knots over the windfall.

Individuals who share my money scripts are vulnerable to squandering any sudden wealth they may encounter. What is particularly insidious about these money avoidance scripts (and the nature of the squandering) is that such individuals will often get rid of the wealth by being generous to others. They will help out any family or friends or charities that seem to be "more" deserving of the money, until they eventually run out.

In my case, I used my father's life insurance money to give to charity, to fund my sons' 529 plan college savings accounts, and to add to my retirement account. As I made these decisions, I congratulated myself on using the money in ways Dad would have approved of—he was a damn fine financial planner who preached the importance of saving, investing, and giving. What I could hardly acknowledge to myself was that I felt a sense of profound relief at having the money leave my direct control. Once the money was tied up in financial ventures that I thought would get Dad's seal of approval, I was no longer distressed by the sensation that I was "enjoying" money I had done nothing to earn.

My financial choices for Dad's life insurance money do not fit the traditional definition of "squandering," but my relief at divesting myself of the money means I can't claim that my choices were entirely rational.

Overcoming the urge to squander wealth is very difficult to do on your own. It is often in your best interests to partner with a trusted financial adviser who is willing to protect you from your own urges to squander the money. If you do not already have a financial adviser whom you trust, I offer advice on how to find one in Chapter 4 of my book *The 5 Years Before You Retire: Retirement Planning When You Need It the Most*.

Risky Investments

A common money avoidance belief is the sense that you don't or can't understand money or investments. Many money avoiders who carry such a belief will refrain from making any money or investment choices as a form of financial denial. Still others, however, will engage in risky investment strategies because their money avoidance script makes them believe that they do not understand finances. The following example illustrates how it often plays out:

Lanny carries the money avoidant belief that he's too stupid to understand finances, and he feels ashamed that he doesn't do anything with his money beyond putting it in a savings account. But the gazingus pin market is hot right now, and everywhere Lanny turns, there's another news story about small-time investors making huge gains pretty much overnight. With the way prices keep rising on gazingus pins, it seems that even an idiot like him can't lose—so Lanny decides to invest all of his savings. He would hate to compound his money stupidity by missing out on a sure bet.

Lanny's investments initially do well, but the gazingus pin market was close to the top of a bubble when he invested. Not long after his initial investment, the gazingus pin bubble bursts, and Lanny sees the value of his investments cut in half. Discouraged and angry at himself, Lanny liquidates his investments and puts the money back into savings. He's now absolutely sure that he's too stupid to understand finances and that it was ridiculous for him to try.

Lanny's investment problems have nothing to do with his intelligence. As a matter of fact, savvy investing has far more to do with behavior than intelligence. What's really going on with Lanny is that his money avoidance script kept him from educating himself on investing. His conviction that he was incapable of learning more about money led him to make risky investment decisions, and when those decisions cost him money, his beliefs about his own lack of intelligence were reinforced.

Investing Is Easier Than You Think

Getting into the nitty-gritty of savvy investing is beyond the scope of this book, but I do want to touch on the subject of investments. Many people believe that it's necessary to have an MBA to truly understand investing, but that is not the case. Remember that it is in the financial industry's best interest to make investing seem too complicated for the average person to understand. But regular people can do well for themselves by following three simple investment rules:

1. Plan to invest for the long term, meaning *at least* ten or more years. This will allow your investments to ride out market fluctuations.

2. Base your investing on statistical analyses rather than predictions. You can do this by investing in index funds.

3. Choose index funds with low fees (under 2 percent, or lower) so that your returns are not eaten up by fees.

For further information about how to be a savvy investor, I invite you to read Chapter 3: "Demystifying Your Investments" in my book *Choose Your Retirement: Find the Right Path to Your New Adventure.*

MONEY WORSHIP AND MONEY STATUS PROBLEMS

The money scripts from the worship and status categories tend to overlap, which means money worshipers and money status-seekers are vulnerable to similar types of financial problems.

Overspending

Spending more than you can afford is one of the most common financial problems plaguing Americans. There are any number of reasons why overspending is such an issue for so many of us—including how credit is easy for most people to obtain and that society sends us constant messages to spend, spend, spend. But overspending is often also a symptom of certain types of money scripts. In particular, individuals who believe they deserve the best in life, those who tie their self-worth to their net worth and/or their possessions, those who believe money would solve all their problems, and those who believe they must project an image of success in order to become successful are all more susceptible to overspending.

Overspending can take different forms. Some overspenders indulge in "retail therapy" after a bad day, whereas others would never consider shopping to be a stress antidote but instead own a house and/or a car whose payments they can barely afford.

Theoretically, overspending is one of the easier financial problems to correct because what you spend is entirely within your control. No one will hold a gun to your head and force you to spend money to purchase something you can't afford. However, the society we live in makes it very difficult to disengage from overspending. Not only does society encourage us to spend, but the people around us can also exert pressure (from the subtle to the overt) to keep us spending like we always have. This is similar to the struggles facing a recovering alcoholic who is surrounded by both liquid temptations and enabling friends and family. We will talk about concrete ways to deal with overspending at the end of this chapter.

Financial Enabling/Dependency

These behaviors are two sides of the same coin. Financial enabling is providing monetary help to others that allows them to avoid taking responsibility for the consequences of their money choices. Financial dependency is allowing yourself to be financially taken care of so that you do not have to face the consequences of your actions.

Financial enabling often stems from money scripts that conflate money with happiness. Individuals with such scripts want to make their loved ones happy, and so they spend money to protect their dependents from facing their responsibilities. A very common example of financial enabling is when parents sacrifice their retirement savings in order to send their children to college (or alternatively, pay for their child's wedding). Often, this means that the adult children may not have to foot the bill for their entire education (or nuptials), but they are then on the hook for taking care of their elderly parents several decades later.

Of course, the enabling/dependency cycle can be even more pernicious than paying for an education or a wedding. For instance, consider the mother who pays for a replacement car after her adult son totals his car while driving drunk. The mother may think that she needs to bail him out of this situation in order to help him get back on track. However, if buying a new car insulates her son from experiencing the consequences of his actions, and he continues to make financially and personally destructive decisions, she is enabling his irresponsibility.

Financial Abuse

Financial dependency is also a major hallmark of financial abuse. For instance, in an emotionally or physically abusive marriage, the abuser may also take complete control of the finances and prevent his spouse from working outside the home or opening credit or banking accounts in her own name. This is one of the reasons why it is so important for everyone to feel competent to handle his or her own finances so that financial independence can never be completely taken away.

On the other side of the coin, financially dependent individuals may believe that there will always be someone they can turn to for money, or that being a good person means that their needs will always be taken care of. But those who allow themselves to become financially dependent are also more likely to believe that they should not buy something unless it is the best, according to Dr. Klontz's research. Individuals who suffer from financial dependency are often afraid of dealing with the consequences of their actions, and so they continue to depend on others for money even as they feel resentful of their dependent position.

Workaholism

If you believe that more money leads to more happiness or that poor people are lazy, then you are likely very susceptible to workaholism. You will either work hard in order to chase the happiness you feel sure is just around the next pay raise, or in order to relieve yourself of the fear that you must be lazy because you don't earn more.

The classic example of workaholism is the hard-working father who never spends time with this family because he feels as if he must show his love by being a good provider. However, there are many different stripes of workaholism. For instance, a new mother with the money script that "poor people are lazy" may find that she spends her unpaid maternity leave cleaning the house top to bottom, starting a new garden, and enrolling her newborn in back-to-back mother-and-infant classes in order to avoid the feeling that she is being lazy. She engages in a great deal of activity, when she could simply be bonding with her new child, just to prove to herself that she's not lazy.

As with overspending, workaholism is both common and encouraged in our society. Just look at the number of books, blogs, and podcasts devoted to productivity to see that workaholism has a strong hold on our culture. The cultural approval of workaholism makes it that much more difficult for individuals to change their workaholic ways.

MONEY VIGILANCE PROBLEMS

Though money vigilance scripts are often helpful for keeping finances in order, there are some common stress-inducing problems that the money vigilant face.

Underspending

It's rare that a personal finance writer will call out not spending enough as a financial problem, considering that spending less than you earn is the cornerstone of financial health. However, there is certainly a point at which working to avoid spending money becomes a financial problem. The Charles Dickens character Ebenezer Scrooge embodies the problems of underspending; despite his great wealth he lives in a small house that he refuses to heat adequately and he eats very little to save money. His life is empty and joyless.

Underspending is not just about being a miser. It can also cost you money. For instance, an underspender might keep the same pair of running shoes for several years, resulting in a bad repetitive-use injury because of the wear on her old shoes. To avoid paying the $100 she would have spent on a pair of good running shoes, she may be out hundreds (or thousands) of dollars in healthcare to fix her injury, as well as whatever amount of money she will lose by not being able to work while she recovers.

Underspending is generally related to either maximizing (that is, the overvaluing of opportunity costs as we discussed back in Chapter 2), or the anxiety that there is not enough money, or both. In Chapter 2, we discussed ways of combatting maximizing behavior, and we will talk about how to deal with financially anxious underspending at the end of this chapter.

Hoarding

All of us have a little trouble parting with items if we're not sure we might need them again in the future. It feels like a terrible waste of money when you need to rebuy something that you got rid of. But individuals with money vigilant scripts like *It's important to save for a rainy day* and *Money should be saved and not spent* are more vulnerable than most to the problem of hoarding things they can't use and don't need.

Hoarding may allow someone to feel as if he is saving money by holding on to anything he might need in the future. The hoarder is not considering the time cost of his hoarding. When he needs something, he will either have to spend hours (or days, depending upon the scale of his hoarding) searching for the item—or he will have to go out and purchase another one if he is in any kind of time crunch.

Hoarding behavior is common among individuals who have lived through times of traumatic privation, such as war, or economic depression, and it can often be passed down to subsequent generations.

Working Around Your Destructive Money Scripts

Many of the destructive financial issues we have discussed throughout this chapter have their roots in deep-seated thought patterns and mindsets that take time and effort to dislodge. I will end this chapter with a journaling exercise that can help you to reframe some of the thought patterns to which you are most vulnerable. Before we get to that, though, I'd like to offer you some small, practical methods for combatting your destructive money scripts.

Freezing Your Credit Card

Personal finance advice is full of little tricks that force you to behave. One of the old chestnuts of financial advice is to freeze your credit card in a block of ice so that it's impossible to make an impulse purchase on credit. While this advice may sound old-fashioned, it's actually very astute. The time it would take you to thaw out your credit card provides you with enough emotional distance to rethink an impulsive purchase.

COMBATTING MONEY AVOIDANCE SCRIPTS

Money avoiders generally need to find productive ways to ignore their money and put barriers in place between themselves and the temptation to give money away:

1. Set up automatic transfers of your money to savings and/ or retirement accounts. Money avoiders often don't want to think about money, so using automated transfers allows them to productively avoid money decisions. Chapter 11 contains detailed methods for setting up your budget and your automatic transfers if you want to avoid thinking about your money.

2. If you know that you are likely to panic if you see the balance of your investments go down, only look at your investment summaries twice a year, which is more than sufficient to keep your accounts balanced. For all summaries that come in the mail, put a date on the outer envelope that represents when you can look at it—and don't touch it until then. For the accounts you can access online, choose an unusual password (but be sure you know your security questions) to keep yourself from checking too often.

3. Tell family and friends who ask for money that they need to talk to you and your financial adviser. (This is also helpful for money worshipers or status seekers who struggle with financial enabling.) You may have trouble saying no to family requests for money. If you commit to making financial decisions with the help of a trusted adviser, then you will have not only given yourself an ally in achieving and maintaining financial health, you will have also added a layer of difficulty to your family member's request. Often, making the act of asking for money slightly harder is enough to keep the moochers at bay.

COMBATTING MONEY WORSHIP AND MONEY STATUS SCRIPTS

Since money worshipers and status seekers both struggle with overspending in an attempt to buy happiness, it is important for individuals with those scripts to put barriers in place to keep them from unnecessary spending:

1. Institute a twenty-four-hour rule for financial decisions. Both con artists and salespeople give their sales a sense of urgency, whether they're selling a stake in a tin mine in Bolivia or a deluxe shiatsu massage chair. Forcing yourself to wait until your excitement has cooled down will help you look rationally at a purchase that—in the moment—seems to solve all your problems. There are two ways to institute such a rule: agree to discuss all purchases over $50 (or $100) with your spouse or get in the habit of only carrying cash when you leave the house.

2. Use a rubber band to wrap a folded-down 8½" × 11" sheet of paper around each one of your credit and debit cards. On the paper, write the following questions:

- Do I need to buy this?
- Do I need to buy it now?
- Will purchasing this item help me reach my goals?
- What else could I do with this money?

Though the questions can help you to think through each purchase, the simple irritation of unwrapping your method of payment from a full-size sheet of paper can be enough to keep your buying in check.

3. Remove your credit card information from all of your favorite online retailers. When you can go from coveting an item to purchasing it with a single click, it is far too easy to spend money. Remove the "convenience" of having your credit card information stored, and you will give yourself a small barrier between you and mindless purchasing online.

COMBATTING MONEY VIGILANCE SCRIPTS

Underspending is a problem for the money vigilant, not just because it leads to living in a level of discomfort that is unnecessary, but also because it can waste a great deal of money. If you tend to underspend on yourself, precommitting to necessary spending can help you combat your reluctance to spend:

1. Sign up for a healthcare flexible spending account. These accounts allow you to set aside pretax dollars from your paycheck to use for medical expenses. Since these types of accounts are use-it-or-lose-it plans, enrolling in such an account will give you the motivation you need to actually go to the doctor when you need healthcare, because you would otherwise be wasting the money.

2. Buy nonrefundable gift cards for purchases for yourself. Similar to the flexible spending account idea, precommitting to a purchase for yourself by buying a gift card will force you to make the needed purchase when your money vigilance script is pushing you not to. In addition, you can often find nonrefundable gift cards at a discount at online gift card exchanges such as Gift Card Granny (www.giftcardgranny.com) and Cardpool (www.cardpool.com), which will satisfy other aspects of your money vigilant personality.

Journaling to Change Your Mindset

When it comes to several of the destructive financial behaviors we discussed in this chapter—including financial denial, overspending, financial enabling/dependency, workaholism, underspending, and hoarding—there is only so much that practical "life hack" type tips can do to help you. These issues represent financial viewpoints that are often global for the individuals who struggle with them. For instance, a workaholic who tries to reduce her workload may struggle with how to show love for her family, her own feelings of laziness and/or worthlessness, and a sense of anxiety over her bank balance *all at the same time*. She has to work on changing three different aspects of her money mindset just to handle this particular issue.

Fortunately, researchers have found that you can consciously edit your money scripts. Anne Kates Smith, senior editor at *Kiplinger*, reports that journaling can be an excellent method for rewriting harmful money scripts:

> [Jot] down thoughts that pop up in any given financial situation . . . Journaling slows the process, and it captures patterns in your thinking. Once you're aware of the patterns, you can work on changing them. . . . If you tend to panic when the stock market plunges, for instance, one of your scripts might be something like *I'm going to lose everything!* Instead, remind yourself that stocks rise and fall, and while you may lose some money, you have a plan and a diversified portfolio.

Literally editing your thoughts on the page will do a great deal to edit them in your mind. When the panicked investor crosses out her first thought of *I'm going to lose everything!* and writes the reminder that the market fluctuates, then she is reinforcing the new thought patterns.

With each destructive money script you capture through your journaling, take some time to figure out how you would like to rewrite it. As situations that trigger your money script come up, use your journal to edit your own thoughts. Slowly, you will start to take on the improved, rewritten script—which will reduce your financial stress and improve your financial decisions.

Chapter Seven Takeaways

1. There are four categories of money scripts: money avoidance, money worship, money status, and money vigilance.

2. Money scripts are neither "right" nor "wrong." They are simply the financial lens through which you view the world.

3. Depending upon which types of money scripts you carry, you may be vulnerable to different types of disordered financial behavior.

4. There are practical methods for bypassing your destructive money scripts even while you are doing the work necessary to uproot your most damaging unconscious money behavior.

5. You can literally rewrite your destructive money scripts through regular journaling.

CHAPTER EIGHT

The Destructive Nature of *Should* and *Deserve*

WHAT YOU'LL LEARN IN THIS CHAPTER

- We use the word should to shame ourselves for the choices we make. This shame causes us great financial stress without changing our behavior in any productive or meaningful way.
- We justify poor financial behavior by claiming we deserve whatever we are doing. This means we overlook or underestimate the consequences of pursuing the things we believe we are entitled to.
- A healthy attitude toward money begins by ridding ourselves of the shame of should and the entitlement of deserve.

"Stop shoulding on yourself."
—*Albert Ellis*

During my freshman year in college, one of my dormmates noticed one night that every sentence uttered by any of us hanging out in the student lounge always started with the same two words:

"I should have started this essay last week."

"I should go to bed."

"I should be able to figure out this formula."

"I should not have skipped that lecture."

"I should call my mom."

At the time my fellow college student made the observation, I just thought it was a funny side effect of pursuing higher education. What I didn't realize then was that the word "should" represents a destructive pattern of thinking that many of us follow throughout our adult lives.

The word "should" does not represent situations as they are but as they could be in some ideal world. For instance, I tend to should on myself about my cleaning habits. I have long resisted the common-sense suggestion that you keep cleaning supplies where you use them. Instead, all of my spritzes, sprays, rags, and the like are in the kitchen under the sink. So when I need to clean the bathroom, I have to schlep the cleaning products from the kitchen in order to do so—which can put a damper on my enthusiasm to regularly clean the bathroom.

My resistance to keeping some cleaning supplies in the bathroom stems from a should statement I tell myself: "It's ridiculous to have cleaning supplies in every room of the house. I should be able to just grab it all from the kitchen when I need it." I resist the idea of buying extra cleaning supplies to stow in the places where I need them because in some part of my mind I think that I should be able to keep my house clean without it being easy.

It's important to recognize just how much shame is baked in to such should statements. I feel ashamed of the fact that my cleaning habits leave something to be desired, and rather than make cleaning easy for myself so I no longer need to feel ashamed, I construct a should statement about how I ought to behave. This should statement prevents me from making it easier to clean, which makes it even more difficult for me to act in a way that will relieve my feelings of shame. This is how should statements become a shame loop.

In most cases, should is not only a word you can delete from your vocabulary, but also it's one that can hold you back from achieving your goals, financial or otherwise. Here are the three ways that should can cause shame and financial distress:

PAST SHOULDS

These are the kinds of should statements that make you feel ashamed of past decisions. These types of statements often come from other people who delight in giving you *coulda-shoulda-woulda* advice that would have been wonderfully helpful to you sometime in the past.

Within the personal finance sphere, you will find many individuals who are happy to shame you for your past financial decisions. For instance, you might hear a financial guru say:

"You cosigned a loan with your shiftless brother-in-law and are now stuck paying off his debt? Too bad! You should never have cosigned a loan unless you were prepared to take on the debt solo."

or:

"You didn't start saving for retirement until you were in your forties or fifties or later? Too bad! You should have started earlier to take advantage of compound interest."

or:

"You double majored in English and French Literature (ahem) and now you can't find a job or pay your student loans? Too bad! You should have majored in something that guaranteed a lucrative post-college career."

It's not entirely clear what the so-called experts who proffer such advice expect you to do with their words of wisdom. Other than hang our heads and mumble, "You're right, of course," there is absolutely nothing we can do with this kind of advice—which is why it is worse than useless. Once someone proclaims that you did something in the past that you should have done differently, you are still stuck with your current problem, and you feel bad about yourself, to boot.

It gets even more problematic when we internalize those past should statements, such that we feel ashamed of those past choices even with no third party generously pointing out the mistake. When this occurs, you might spend a great deal of time beating yourself up for past choices and feeling as though there is nothing you can do to fix issues in the future. For instance, if you feel as if you should have started saving for retirement earlier, it's easy for you to conclude that there is no point in starting now since you are already so far behind. Of course, that kind of thinking just hurts your finances more.

Combatting Past Shoulds

Feeling shame over things you did in the past is a form of the sunk cost fallacy. As you'll recall from Chapter 2, sunk costs are the time, money, or resources that have already been spent and cannot be recouped. The sunk cost fallacy is the mistake we make wherein we value sunk costs over opportunity costs. For instance, a newly minted doctor who realizes during his first year of residency that he hates medicine might be tempted to continue his career regardless, because he doesn't want to have wasted all the time, effort, and money he spent becoming an MD. But this temptation might cause him to overlook the fact that overvaluing his sunk costs will keep him stuck in a career he hates.

Feeling as though you should have done something differently in the past is related to such a sunk cost fallacy. You are overvaluing the past decision and allowing it to affect your current emotional state and possibly even your current decisions.

For instance, the individual who should not have cosigned a loan with her brother-in-law may be so stuck on her sunk cost decision that she does not explore the options available to her in her current position. She spends her energy beating herself up about the past decision, rather than figuring out if there are any ways to refinance the loan or recoup the payments from her brother-in-law.

Anyone who is hoping to end financial stress must deal with her financial situation as it is, not as it might have been. As we discussed in Chapter 2, there are two helpful thought patterns to adopt to end the shame of past should statements:

1. *Imagine you just woke up with amnesia.* Luciano Passuello, blogger at Litemind (https://litemind.com), came up with the term "zero-based thinking" to describe this thought exercise. Passuello suggests you imagine you just woke up in your current situation with amnesia,

without any memory of how you got there. That allows your current decision to reside wholly in the present, and helps you not to focus on what you could have done differently in the past.

2. *Proudly admit your mistakes.* The shame you feel about bad decisions stems from you having made a mistake in the past. Owning up to mistakes, and even proudly admitting them, can help you to recognize that regretting a mistake does not need to make you feel ashamed. Mistakes in your past are past, and moving forward while acknowledging them can feel liberating.

PRESENT SHOULDS

Present shoulds often start with the words "I should be able to . . ." Unlike the past should statements that often come from "helpful" experts, present shoulds usually generate from within. They are the stories we tell ourselves when we do not live up to some sort of internal ideal for behavior.

For instance, I am not a home improvement do-it-yourselfer. For many years, I felt pretty terrible about my lack of DIY skills. Not only is that kind of skill set an important part of living frugally, but it also represents a type of independent confidence that I have always wanted to possess. When faced with a home maintenance problem, I would find myself thinking, "I should be able to fix the leaking faucet by myself. I'm smart, frugal, and independent—so what's wrong with me?"

This kind of should statement shames you for being exactly who you are. In my case, after years of berating myself about it, I came to realize that I do not have an interest in or an aptitude for most DIY skills. This made me feel ashamed, since my expectations for frugality and independence did not align with my own skill set.

These types of should statements are very common in finance. Many people believe they should be able to:

- Save a certain percentage of their money
- Stick to their budget
- Stop overdrawing their account

- Start comparison shopping/coupon clipping
- Personally take care of home maintenance
- Be good at handling money

And these are just the tip of the "should be able to" financial iceberg.

What's most pernicious about these types of should statements is that they keep you from finding solutions. For instance, someone who beats himself up for overdrawing his account starts with the assumption that he should be able to check in on his finances on a regular basis to make sure he doesn't overdraw his account again. However, just the feeling that he should be on top of his finances to avoid overdrafts doesn't change the fact that checking his account balance is the furthest thing from his mind. Thinking "I should be able to do this!" keeps him from finding another solution—such as having his bank send him daily text or e-mail alerts with his balance.

This is why it's so important to recognize your own limitations and plan for them. The man struggling with overdrafts can acknowledge that he can't stop overdrawing his account. Once he recognizes that, he can work within that truth instead of trying over and over to be someone he is not.

Combatting Present Should Statements

To keep your present should statements from derailing your finances, you need to reframe the statement in your own head, accounting for your limitation. When you find yourself thinking, "I should be able to _____," don't allow that to be the end of your thought. Instead, complete the thought productively by adding, "but I can't—so now what?" Admitting to yourself that you can't (or won't) do something frees you to be able to ask how to remedy the situation.

In my own case, my lifelong belief that I should be able to handle DIY homeowner maintenance and repair meant that I was never completely prepared for a problem. Since I believed I should be able to handle things myself, I did not have money set aside for contractors, but I also had no skills or resources to call upon when there was an issue. Then I changed my thought pattern: "I should be able to handle home repairs myself, but I can't—so now what?" Once the thought was complete, the answer become obvious: I needed to set money aside for home maintenance. From there, I could think through how much I would need to set aside to afford the inevitable maintenance and repair issues and decide what cuts I was willing to make to my budget to make sure the savings account stayed full. I now treat the home maintenance and repair savings account like a bill, setting aside a chunk of money each month. This allows me to feel less stress about home maintenance costs and reduces the shame about my choices and abilities.

Shouldn't I Be Able to Do That?

Upon reading this section, you might wonder if I am suggesting that you are under no obligation to improve yourself. After all, there are excellent reasons why you might want to learn better money skills, avoid overdrafts, become more self-sufficient with home maintenance chores, and the like.

It's important to remember that there is no reason why you cannot accept who you are while also working on self-improvement. In fact, without the self-acceptance and the corresponding work you do to protect yourself from your own worst impulses, it is next to impossible to improve your skills. I am much more likely to learn home maintenance skills when the stakes are low (that is, when the basement is not flooding while I frantically search YouTube for how-to videos). Recognizing that you can't do something means that you allow yourself to lower the stakes in order to learn the skill.

FUTURE SHOULDS

Future should statements are often about the things you need to be doing but aren't. For instance, my husband switched jobs in 2010 and neglected to roll over his 401(k) at the time. Ever since then, he has been periodically reminding himself, "I should roll over my 401(k)."

Yes, he absolutely should. He is not wrong to come back to this should statement on a regular basis.

This is what makes future should statements different from past and present should statements. Future should statements often represent a course of action that you actually should follow. You just aren't doing it yet. While future should statements can cause you to feel shame—for not completing the task yet—they do not tend to represent counterproductive, shame-based thought patterns that hold you back.

Dealing with Future Should Statements

The issue with future should statements is their simplicity. When my husband thinks, "I should roll over my 401(k)," the thought sounds as simple and easy as "I should pick up milk on the way home." But most future should statements represent a complex task that requires information, effort, resources, or time that you may not currently have. Your should statement does not recognize those missing items, and so it just continues to sit on your mental to-do list as if it were a single, simple action you could take.

The Getting Things Done (GTD) program, created by productivity expert David Allen and featured in his book *Getting Things Done: The Art of Stress-Free Productivity*, offers a solution to the problem of future should statements. The GTD philosophy is based upon five steps for productivity:

1. *Capture everything.* This means write down (or otherwise record) everything that you need to do. When my husband finds himself thinking, "I should roll over my 401(k)," he should write that task down rather than let it continue to rattle around in his head.

2. *Clarify what you have to do.* This is where you de-simplify your should statement. Once my husband has written down, "Roll over 401(k)," he will need to break down that task into actionable steps so that he has thought through what he needs to do to complete the task.

3. *Organize the actionable steps.* Once you recognize what you need to do, you can determine each step you need to take and when. For instance, my husband's first actionable step might be calling his previous employer's human resources department to get the necessary paperwork for a rollover.

4. *Review your task list.* Since completing your future should statements may take multiple tasks spread out over several days, it's important to look over your actionable steps regularly to make sure you are making progress. Once my husband has received the paperwork from his previous employer, he will need to recall what the next step is and not let the paperwork marinate on his desk. Unless you are regularly reviewing your task lists, it's easy to lose track of any multistep tasks you are trying to complete.

5. *Engage.* Follow your action steps until your should statement is complete.

In addition to the complexity that keeps many of your future shoulds from being completed, there are also sometimes-invisible stumbling blocks keeping us from finishing the tasks we know we need to do. In the next chapter, we will discuss how small passive barriers often keep us from finishing these sorts of actions, and we will complete an exercise designed to help you get to the bottom of your procrastination.

"Deserve" Is a Dangerous Word

Whether we are considering a lavish vacation, a new gadget, a fancy car, or a dinner out, we often use the justification "I *deserve* this!" to excuse the spending. We think of all the hard work we have done, the sacrifices we have made, and the lack of acknowledgment for that work and those sacrifices. We decide that we are entitled to whatever splurge we are considering—because we deserve it.

The first problem with this attitude is that whatever you deserve is necessarily defined as something you lack. Whether you feel you deserve a raise at work or a lavish vacation, you are placing yourself in a position where what you already have is not enough. This is neither a recipe for happiness nor a path out of financial stress. Instead, it will make you feel resentful, whether or not you splurge on the thing you feel you deserve.

In addition, using the deserve justification can be disastrous if you are struggling with your finances. After all, what do these "deserving" purchases really provide you? A momentary sense of satisfaction, perhaps. After that, you are likely to face a maxed-out credit card or an overdrawn bank account. "Deserve" enough purchases, and you might find yourself fielding calls from collection agencies or visits from repossession agents. All of this adds to your financial stress.

COMBATTING THE DANGER OF DESERVE

What do you deserve? If you think that material possessions or experiences are the things you deserve, then you've got it backwards.

What you deserve is freedom from financial stress.

While purchases may feel luxurious in the moment, they will land you in a pile of financial stress that you don't deserve. Enjoying a stress-free financial life will feel far better than any new car ever could.

How do you combat the insidious nature of the word "deserve"? The trick is to take time to feel grateful for what is already in your life.

As we discussed in Chapter 5, when we explored the issue of hedonic adaptation, expressing gratitude can help you feel more optimistic and happier. In addition, according to research into gratitude practices, individuals who regularly express gratitude are less likely to judge success in terms of possessions, and they are more likely to make progress toward important personal goals.

When you are struggling with the sense that you deserve something, take a moment to jot down a list of things in your life that you are grateful for. This exercise can help you remember how full your life already is, which will help you put your desired purchase in context.

Chapter Eight Takeaways

1. Should statements tend to be shame-based and counterproductive.

2. Past should statements make you feel ashamed of decisions you made in the past and can harm your ability to make good decisions in the present. Admit to your mistakes and move forward with the situation as it currently is, rather than berate yourself for your past screw-ups.

3. Present should statements make you feel ashamed of who you are because you do not live up to some ideal. Combat these shaming statements by recognizing your limitations and working within them.

4. Future should statements are often tasks that need to be done. Don't let them be stray thoughts, but capture the ideas and break down exactly what you need to do to complete the tasks.

5. The word "deserve" is dangerous because it defines success as something you lack.

6. Regularly practicing gratitude can help you overcome the destructive nature of the word "deserve."

CHAPTER NINE

Small Barriers

WHAT YOU'LL LEARN IN THIS CHAPTER

- Small barriers are the often-invisible obstacles standing between you and your financial goals.
- Small barriers are either active or passive.
- Both active and passive barriers can keep you from your goals, but it is the passive barriers that are more difficult to identify and overcome.
- You can use small barriers to your advantage to keep your financial behavior on the straight and narrow.

So far in this section of the book, we have discussed some of the deep-seated psychological reasons behind your financial distress. However, not all financial problems have such deep roots. Sometimes, relatively simple things might be keeping you from the stress-free financial life you want to live.

For instance, economists have long lamented that poor families will often forgo filling out the paperwork for college financial aid for their children. These families are potentially leaving tens of thousands of dollars of financial aid on the table. One might conclude that the parents either don't care about education or they don't care about their children.

Nothing could be further from the truth.

The reason these families don't fill out financial aid paperwork is because *the forms are too complicated.* The Free Application for Federal Student Aid (FAFSA) clocks in at more than 100 questions regarding income, assets, and expenses. In fact, according to economist Judith Scott-Clayton, writing for *The New York Times*, the FAFSA "is longer and more complicated than the [IRS Form] 1040A and 1040EZ, the tax forms filed by a majority of taxpayers." Faced with a form that makes filing taxes look easy, the very families that most need financial help for college are the ones likely to procrastinate on the FAFSA until it's too late.

The amount of time necessary to hunt up financial information and fill out a boring and overwhelming form is a small barrier when compared to the amount of money available for low-income families who do complete the form—but it's large enough to discourage a number of people from applying for aid and even going to college altogether.

That is the problem with small barriers. They are generally surmountable, but only if you take the time and effort to identify them and leap over them. Until you get over your small barriers, you will avoid doing the simple and basic things that you *already know you need to do* in order to improve your finances.

Active Barriers versus Passive Barriers

You might think that using the term "small barrier" is just another way of describing procrastination or laziness. However, that is a very reductive and self-shaming way of looking at real (but small) problems that keep you from doing the things that will improve your finances and your life.

As we discussed in Chapter 8, it is very easy to get hung up on what you *should* be able to do and beat yourself up for not living up to that expectation. After all, there is no secret to making good financial decisions. You know that you need to set money aside for a rainy day, save up for large purchases, plan ahead for your retirement, and avoid mindless spending. The fact that you struggle with these simple (but not easy) steps to financial improvement may feel like a personal failing of some kind. However, in many cases, what you are confronting is a small barrier that you don't even realize is there. Such small barriers can trip you up in many areas of your life.

For instance, you have probably fallen victim to a small barrier sometime in the past twenty-four hours. Do any of these behaviors sound familiar?

- The dishwasher is full of clean dishes that need to be unloaded, so you leave the breakfast dishes in the sink.
- You can't find the remote control, so you keep watching the nineteen-year-old episode of Friends you've already seen more times than you can count.
- The cantaloupe you bought at the farmers' market is rotting away in the refrigerator because you have not cut it up to eat.
- The permission slip for your child's field trip is still sitting on the kitchen counter a week after it came home because you didn't have a pen handy when your child first gave it to you.

Author and blogger Ramit Sethi, whom we met back in Chapter 1, coined the term "small barrier" to describe these difficult-to-identify obstacles. On his blog I Will Teach You to Be Rich (www.iwillteachyoutoberich.com), Sethi explains that there are two types of these barriers: active and passive.

- Active barriers are physical things that keep you from doing what you want. For instance, the still-loaded dishwasher is a physical barrier keeping you from cleaning up your breakfast dishes. Similarly, a person telling you that your idea will never work or that you are too inexperienced/old/lazy/undereducated/etc. to do what you plan is an active barrier. Such barriers can be hard to identify but easy to fix. Once you recognize what is standing in your way, you can make these barriers go away—by unloading the dishwasher or avoiding negative people, for instance.
- Passive barriers are things whose *absence* actually stops you from getting things done. Such passive barriers are things that don't exist but that make whatever you are trying to do much more difficult. As an example, Sethi cites the trivial passive barrier of not having a stapler at your desk. It can be frustrating several times a

day to be missing this basic office tool, and it could potentially get in the way of your workflow.

For a bigger passive barrier issue, look no further than the low-income families who do not fill out the FAFSA. They may not have the necessary financial information to fill out the form. The information is available somewhere, but because it is not immediately at hand, keeps some low-income families from completing the FAFSA.

According to Sethi, passive barriers are harder to recognize, since determining what you lack is tougher to figure out than determining what is actively in the way. This means passive barriers are harder to fix.

Passive barriers are a consistent problem for individuals trying to improve their finances. For instance, according to a 2006 *Harvard Magazine* article, "In a typical American firm, it takes a new employee a median time of two to three *years* to enroll [in the company's retirement plan]." For the most part, American employees do not avoid enrollment because they are lazy, uninformed, or unmotivated. They drag their feet because enrolling in a 401(k) is complex and requires multiple decisions, each of which may require information or time that the employees feel they are lacking.

The good news is that policymakers have recognized that small barriers are keeping people from making the best decisions for their retirement. In particular, the Pension Protection Act of 2006 provided employers with the statutory authority to automatically enroll new employees in retirement plans. It has worked—according to a study by the National Bureau of Economic Research, participation in defined con-tribution employer retirement plans increased to more than 85 percent for all employees (no matter their length of tenure) after implementa-tion of automatic enrollment. Prior to auto enrollment, participation rates ranged from 26 to 43 percent after six months of tenure, and 57 to 69 percent after three years.

However, enrollment in a retirement plan is only the first of several decisions that can be thwarted by a small barrier. Kelley Holland of CNBC reported in 2015 that "employees participating in auto enroll-ment tend to contribute less than people who sign up for 401(k) plans on their own, often because their employers set a low default contribution level." This is happening because there are small barriers keeping workers from learning more about their retirement plans and increasing their contributions to them. There is only so much that public policy can do to remove small barriers to financial success.

Retirement is only one aspect of finance where small barriers keep people from achieving their goals. This is why it is so important for you to figure out exactly what barriers are keeping *you* from making the best financial decisions for *your* life. To do this, let's return to the exercise from Chapter 1: The Five Whys.

The Five Whys

As you'll recall from Chapter 1, the Five Whys is a diagnostic tool developed by Sakichi Toyoda of the Toyota Motor Corporation to determine the root causes of engineering problems. In the first chapter of this book, we used the Five Whys to help you figure out what meanings you assign to money. But the Five Whys is also very helpful in identifying the small barriers that are keeping you from your financial goals. Answering the Five Whys can help you figure out either what you are missing to fulfill a financial goal or what is standing in your way. Let's look at a couple of financial problems and use the Five Whys to determine their root causes:

Problem: I haven't set up an appointment with an insurance agent to purchase life insurance.

- Why? I don't have all the information I'll need for the meeting.
- Why? I don't know my beneficiaries' Social Security numbers.
- Why? I don't have my kids' paperwork.
- Why? My ex-wife has it.
- Why? I am uncomfortable calling her for it.

In this example, you know that you need to protect your family with life insurance, but you put off making a call to an agent until "later" because you don't have the necessary information. Since you know you have to do something you don't want to do—namely, call your ex-wife—"later" never actually arrives. You end up procrastinating on an important financial task just because you did not want to make a potentially uncomfortable five-minute phone call.

Let's take a look at another example:

Problem: I decided to change my fund selection for my 401(k) last year, but I still haven't done it.

- Why? I don't know how to make the fund selection change.
- Why? I didn't go to the financial education seminar offered by my company that explained how to manage my 401(k).
- Why? I didn't want my coworkers to see me at the seminar.
- Why? I don't want anyone to know that I need help with my finances.
- Why? It makes me feel stupid to admit that I don't understand finance.

In this example, the real barrier is feeling embarrassed for not understanding finance. Once you recognize that you are embarrassed about your lack of knowledge, you can tackle that problem—either by educating yourself or by asking for confidential help from a trusted adviser. However, without examining the root cause of your procrastination, you're liable to attribute it to laziness or weakness on your part—or even lack of time. Knowing the exact small barrier that is keeping you from your goal means that you can face it head on.

Once you reach the root cause of your procrastination, you may look back and think the small barrier that is stopping you is ridiculous. After all, no matter how embarrassing it might be to admit your ignorance about finances, or how uncomfortable a five-minute phone call to your ex might feel, neither of those things is going to hurt you. Nevertheless, these are the kinds of small barriers that might be keeping you from reaching your financial goals.

Now it's your turn to identify the small barriers in your path. What is keeping you from making the best financial decisions to reduce your financial stress? Sethi recommends that you list five things you would be doing with your finances if you were perfect. This list should focus on actions you would be taking (such as *Save 10 percent of my income*) rather than on the outcomes you would like (such as *Have $1 million in the bank*). For instance, you might list *Roll over my retirement account from the job I left four years ago* or *Refinance my mortgage* or even *Set aside six months' worth of expenses in my emergency fund*.

Quickly jot down the five things you wish you were doing with your finances, but that you consistently procrastinate on.

Worksheet 9-1: What Would I Be Doing with My Finances If I Were Perfect?

....

....

....

....

....

Now that you have identified the five things that you feel you ought to be doing with your money, go through the Five Whys exercise for each one. By the time you reach the fifth why in each case, you'll likely discover the small barrier that is keeping you from doing the work you want to do to improve your financial life.

Please note, however, that getting to the root cause of your money problem can be complex and may take some time. This exercise is laid out simply, but you may find that you need do some deep thinking to get to the bottom of your specific money issues. Do not worry if you feel a little overwhelmed here. Just take your time and be open to the answers that may rise to the surface as you think about the reasons behind the choices you make.

Worksheet 9-2: The Five Whys Times Five

PROBLEM 1: ....
Why? ....
Why? ....
Why? ....
Why? ....
Why? ....

PROBLEM 2: ....
Why? ....
Why? ....
Why? ....
Why? ....
Why? ....

PROBLEM 3: ....
Why? ....
Why? ....
Why? ....
Why? ....
Why? ....

PROBLEM 4: ....
Why? ....
Why? ....
Why? ....
Why? ....
Why? ....

PROBLEM 5: ....
Why? ....
Why? ....
Why? ....
Why? ....
Why? ....

Using Small Barriers to Your Advantage

The intentional use of small barriers is an excellent method for making sure you do the things you truly want to do. Small barriers that you put in place yourself can help you from falling victim to temptation. For instance, a dieter might store Halloween candy purchased for trick-or-treaters in the trunk of his car until the festivities begin, meaning he'd have to walk all the way out to his car—an active barrier—to indulge.

You can use the following three small barriers to your advantage:

ACCOUNTABILITY

A promise to yourself to reduce spending or increase your savings is easily broken. After all, even if you beat yourself up for breaking your promise, there is no real barrier between you and your spending temptation. On the other hand, having to account for your actions to another individual changes the game. This is one reason why accountability partners can be such a boon to individuals struggling with any kind of temptations—from falling off the wagon after getting sober to avoiding spending temptations while paying down debt.

One way to use your accountability partner as a small barrier is to set up a credit card or bank statement alert that goes to you *and* your partner. Many credit card companies and banks offer automated alert systems that will e-mail or text you when your available credit dips below a certain amount or when a large transaction has been charged. This information is very helpful for the cardholder, but it can be an even better motivator if you choose to also send it to your accountability partner. So if you find yourself looking longingly at a gorgeous pair of Manolo Blahniks (for all the guys reading this book, those are shoes) and itching to pull out your credit card, you'll remember that your partner will immediately know about the purchase. The small barrier of having to deal with the social consequences of breaking your promise will make you more likely to keep on walking.

REDUCE ACCESS

Spending temptations are much more pernicious in the modern world, wherein you no longer have to get cash from the bank or ATM before spending your money. Since most of us carry credit or debit cards at all times, we suffer from too-easy access to credit or our money. Blogger J.D. Roth writes about this on his site *Money Boss* (http://moneyboss.com):

> I used to find it hard to build savings. As quickly as I put money away, I spent it. Part of the problem was easy access. My checking account and savings account were held at the same credit union. Eventually, I moved my savings account to a different bank (an online savings account) and established a link between the two. When I got paid, I put my money into savings first. I only moved money to checking when I needed it. This one act made a huge difference to my impulse spending.

In addition to moving your savings account to a different bank, you can reduce access to your money by locking up (or even freezing) your credit cards or by placing your savings in assets that penalize you for early access, such as CDs. You will be able to access the credit card or the money in an emergency, but the lack of easy access will keep you from dipping into the money for anything less serious.

REDUCE OPTIONS

Access to your money is only half the problem with living in a world where most people pay with plastic. The other half is the increase in available options that you have when you are carrying a credit or debit card. For instance, back in the bad old days when an evening on the town meant carrying cash, you would have to weigh your options about getting a third cocktail on Saturday night because it would mean you wouldn't have enough cash on hand to take a taxi home. Your options were limited by the amount of cash you carried.

Intentionally limiting your options is another smart way of using small barriers to keep from buying more than you want. Returning to the habit of carrying cash is one excellent way to do this. (There's a reason why it's on the personal finance experts' greatest hits list.) But you can also find other ways to limit your options. For instance, J.D. Roth got in the habit of walking to the grocery store rather than driving. With an entire car available for storage, he knew he'd be tempted to overspend his grocery budget and fill his home with unhealthy foods. On foot, he was limited by the amount of groceries he could comfortably carry.

What's in Your Way?

Whether we like to admit it or not, all of us have a tendency to drift through our decisions, reverting to habit and allowing minor obstacles to keep us from our goals. But once you start looking at the world in terms of the small barriers that shape so many of our actions, you will be able to avoid unintentional barriers in your own life, and consciously mold your path to better financial decisions by using the power of intentional barriers.

Chapter Nine Takeaways

1. Small barriers often stand in the way of large goals. You must identify these small barriers and surmount them if you want to end your financial stress.

2. There are two types of barriers: active and passive. In the case of financial issues, most small barriers are passive.

3. You must analyze your barriers to find the problem at the root of each one so you can overcome them and move forward.

4. Small barriers can also help you to avoid temptations. Creating accountability, reducing your access to your money, and reducing your options are all small barriers that you can use to improve your financial decisions.

PART FOUR

Achieving a Stress-Free Financial Life

The first three parts of the book helped you to understand why you make money mistakes and offered advice on stopping irrational behaviors. This section is a practical guide for applying the advice in the first three-quarters of the book. Over the next four chapters, you will learn ways to increase the breathing room in your budget, create a budgeting system that works for you, resist temptations, and let go of the financial resentment you might be carrying so you can get to work on improving your own finances.

CHAPTER TEN

Finding Your Breathing Room

WHAT YOU'LL LEARN IN THIS CHAPTER

- Creating some financial breathing room will allow you to act on the advice in this book without feeling overwhelmed by your financial situation.
- Adjusting your tax withholding is an effective and almost immediate method for increasing your take-home pay with every paycheck.
- Negotiating your bills is a relatively quick process that can free up some extra money every month.
- Canceling unused subscriptions can painlessly free up money in your monthly budget.
- Refinancing your mortgage can potentially reduce your monthly mortgage payment.
- Debt consolidation can offer some monthly financial relief.

As we discussed in Chapter 4, living with a scarcity mindset causes you to focus intensely on what you lack, while it also taxes your mental bandwidth. If you have a scarcity mindset, reading all the personal finance and budgeting books in the world will not make it any easier for you to act on their advice. Scarcity captures your mind in such a way that it is exceedingly difficult to get ahead, even if you know exactly what you need to do.

In order to take advantage of the advice in this book, you will need to find some financial breathing room to lessen the effect of scarcity on your brain. While many personal finance books and articles purport to offer their readers actionable ways for finding extra money in a budget, those suggestions are often either stress-inducing (like increasing income through side-hustles), small potatoes (like suggestions on how to reduce your grocery bill), or unrealistic (like suggesting you move to an area with a cheaper cost of living).

The suggestions that follow should offer you real improvements in your monthly cash flow without also increasing your overall stress level or asking you to keep track of the savings you see from switching to generic toilet paper. Though not all of the following suggestions will necessarily work for every reader, implementing any one of them can potentially help you find the breathing room you need to get ahead.

Adjust the Withholding on Your W-4

In Chapter 3, we talked about how the average tax refund in 2016 was $3,120. For the average worker, this breaks down to $260 unnecessarily taken from her monthly wage. Many taxpayers plan on using their tax refunds to pay for indulgences that they otherwise would not be able to afford. Instead, you can put that $260 back into your monthly take-home pay. Doing so may be a better use of the money if it can help relieve your feelings of scarcity and allow you to follow your budget and adjust your money mindset.

You can access that extra money by making a trip to your human resources department to adjust your withholding allowances on your W-4 form.

In order to adjust your withholding and begin seeing larger paychecks you need to complete a few straightforward tasks:

REQUEST A NEW W-4 FROM YOUR HUMAN RESOURCES DEPARTMENT

You filled one of these out when you were first hired, but if you're like most people, you probably haven't changed or updated it since then. You should always make changes to your W-4 when you have a life change—like getting married or divorced, having a child, or buying a house. Even if none of those changes has occurred in your life, you can change your withholding allowances to reduce the amount of money withheld from your paychecks.

Aim for a Modest Refund

If you do decide to adjust your tax withholding to increase your take-home pay, it is a good idea to aim for a modest tax refund each year rather than try to owe nothing and receive nothing back. Aiming for a modest refund means you will not find yourself scrambling to pay a tax bill come April of next year if you happen to make a mistake.

So what qualifies as a modest refund? About $500. Aiming for a $500 refund offers you a decent-sized cushion should you miscalculate anything, but it is not such a large amount of money that you miss out on needed cash in your paychecks. If you are like the average American and received a $3,120 refund this year, adjusting your withholding so that you receive a $500 refund will provide you with an additional $218 per month in your take-home pay.

CALCULATE YOUR WITHHOLDING ALLOWANCES

The more withholding allowances you claim, the less tax is withheld from each of your paychecks. Claiming more allowances on the W-4 often makes many taxpayers nervous, because they fear legal or financial repercussions for getting it wrong. It is very important to remember that the withholding allowances you enter into your W-4 do not determine your tax bill, just how much you pay in taxes per paycheck. That means it is perfectly legal to enter additional withholding allowances on your W-4, provided you only claim the correct number of allowances on your actual tax return. You have every legal right to claim additional withholding allowances on your W-4. The only potential problem you could face by changing your withholding allowances is that you may not have enough tax withheld from your paycheck, which means you might owe Uncle Sam money come April 15. You do not have to worry about triggering an audit or other legal issues based upon what you state on your W-4. In addition, as long as the amount you end up owing at tax time is $1,000 or less, there is no financial penalty for under-withholding. If you aim for a modest return of $500, you have nothing to worry about when you adjust your withholding allowances.

The majority of taxpayers who try to reduce their withholding (and increase their take-home pay) simply want to get their withholding allowances exactly right. These taxpayers can use the IRS withholding calculator to help them determine exactly how many allowances they can take. You can find the calculator on the IRS website (www.irs.gov/individuals/irs-withholding-calculator).

It's also good to remember the common allowances taxpayers can take:

- One allowance if you are single and have only one job.
- One allowance if you have one job and your spouse is not employed.
- One allowance if your income from a second job or your spouse's income is $1,500 or less.
- One allowance if you spend at least $2,000 per year in child or dependent-care expenses and plan to take a tax credit.

DETERMINE HOW THE ALLOWANCES WILL BEST BE SPLIT

If you and your spouse are both working, you will want to figure out how many allowances you are both entitled to as a couple and then divide them between you. Generally, you will want to have the higher-earning spouse claim the allowances, as the reduced withholding will often have a greater impact with a higher salary.

Married couples are more likely than single taxpayers to under-withhold, so it's important to make sure you calculate correctly, especially if this is your first year of married life. The W-4 worksheet offers a second page for married couples, which will help you determine the correct number of allowances to make sure you maximize your take-home pay without generating an unpleasant tax season surprise.

Once you file your new W-4 with your employer, you'll soon see fatter paychecks. It normally takes about a month for the new paperwork to make a difference in your paychecks, although it could happen as quickly as your next pay cycle, depending on your HR department.

Negotiate Your Bills

Though many of us feel a little reluctant to negotiate down our bills, taking the time to call your service providers and ask for better prices can result in savings that range from modest to impressive. Since negotiation is a relatively quick process, it is worth your while to try even if your initial savings are modest. As you grow more comfortable with negotiation, you may find that your requests start to make a big difference in your monthly budget.

There are five common types of bills that can be negotiated, even if you are generally allergic to negotiating:

INTERNET/CABLE SERVICE

Your cable company is both the easiest and most difficult service provider to negotiate with. They are the easiest to negotiate with because they are eager to give price breaks in order to keep their customers. They recognize that there is a great deal of competition out there. On the other hand, cable companies also train their customer service agents to "get to the yes"—i.e., be incredibly pushy. This can make negotiating somewhat stressful.

To successfully negotiate down your cable/Internet bill, make sure you do the following:

- *Know the lowest going rate.* When you call, you should know either what price your provider is offering to new subscribers or the rates offered by the competition. You can use that price as leverage for reducing your bill.
- *Talk to the retention/cancellation department.* Generally, your service provider gives the retention/cancellation department staff the most authority to make deals in order to keep you. The billing department does not have that kind of authority. Being willing to walk away is an important part of successful negotiation, which is why you should contact the retention/cancellation department. This technique is especially powerful if there is an alternate provider in your area to whom you are willing to defect.
- *Call back to verify the price change.* Once you have come to an agreement, write down the new terms and call back within the next day or two to verify that your account reflects the new price. If your service provider made a mistake, you won't otherwise know until the next billing cycle is complete.

CELL PHONE SERVICE

Negotiating your cell phone service can be slightly more difficult than doing so with your cable/Internet provider because of the nature of cell phone contracts. However, it is possible to reduce your cell phone bill if you keep a few important things in mind.

- *Timing is important.* You are more likely to successfully reduce your bill if you negotiate toward the end of your contract, when your provider is desperate to hold on to you.
- *Remind them of your loyalty.* It costs cell phone service providers far more money to gain new customers than it does for them to

keep existing ones. If you remind them of how many years you have been using their service, they are more likely to work with you.

- *Be prepared to actually cancel.* As with cable/Internet service provider negotiations, having some teeth behind your threat to cancel gives you the upper hand in negotiations.
- *Ask to speak to supervisors.* If the customer service representative you speak to says he cannot help you, don't be afraid to ask for a manager.

AUTO INSURANCE

The insurance industry has a number of discounts and savings options available for people who just ask. Call your insurance company and ask for ways to save on your monthly payment. There may be options available—such as signing up for online billing or a safe-driver program—that will save you money with very little (or no) effort on your part. As with your cell phone provider, long-standing loyalty can serve you well in negotiations.

MEDICAL BILLS

Hospitals are set up to negotiate medical bills, so it is worth your while to talk to their billing office about the terms of your payment.

RENT

Even though your rental payment may seem like it's a take-it-or-leave amount, there is often some wiggle room, especially if you are a reliable tenant and have plans to stay where you are for a while. The best way to accomplish this is by asking your landlord for a longer-term lease in exchange for a discount in your rent. That can be a win-win for you both.

Cancel Unused Subscriptions

Many companies make their money through subscription services that their customers no longer use. While most of us are perfectly aware of our subscriptions to Netflix or Stitch Fix, sometimes we forget about subscriptions we have signed up for, and several months (or even years) can go by before we realize that we are still paying $20 a month for a subscription we don't use.

According to a 2013 study by industry analysts Aite Group, consumers spend $14.3 billion on these charges each year. These ongoing fees, known in the industry as gray charges, account for 233 million transactions per year. The charges are legal, and rely on the fact that most people do not pay close attention to their statements. They also rely on consumer apathy, since even the credit and debit card users who discover gray charges often decide that the hassle of canceling outweighs the cost of paying the fees.

The DIY method of canceling unused subscriptions is simple but not necessarily easy: look through your credit card and bank statements to identify the offending gray charges, and call to cancel the unused subscriptions. If you'd rather not spend the time yourself, however, there are two quality apps that will do the work for you—entirely for free.

TRIM

Trim (www.asktrim.com) asks you to register your primary credit cards. The app then uses algorithms to identify recurring payments that can be canceled. It then texts you to ask permission to cancel those subscriptions. Trim takes care of contacting the merchant on your behalf, meaning it will send a template e-mail, make a phone call, or even send certified mail on your behalf to cancel things like old gym memberships, which can be notoriously difficult to wiggle out of. Trim takes security very seriously, so the program uses bank-level security and encryption to keep your information safe.

TRUEBILL

Truebill (www.truebill.com) links to your primary credit card or bank account, then identifies subscriptions that can be canceled. It notifies you of those subscriptions and offers you a one-click cancellation process. According to their promotional literature, the average Truebill user saves $512 per year. Truebill also uses bank-level security and encryption to maintain the security of your financial information.

Refinance Your Mortgage

If you own your home, refinancing your mortgage can be a savvy method for reducing your monthly mortgage payment while also lowering your interest rate. To refinance your home, you will pay off your current mortgage by taking out a new loan at a lower interest rate or a different repayment term. Most refinancers will either save money on their monthly mortgage payment, and/or reduce their interest rate, or reduce their loan term.

Smart refinancing is all about the numbers, so you need to make sure you are well aware of all the costs you could be facing with your refinance. In particular, make sure you know the answers to the following questions:

1. *How will your interest rate change?* As of this writing, average interest rates for refinancing a mortgage hover between 3.5 percent and 4.5 percent. This is great news for any homeowner with a good credit score who purchased his or her home at a rate of 5 percent or higher. In general, refinancing can be worthwhile if you drop your percentage rate by at least half a percentage point.

2. *How will your monthly mortgage payment change?* Since we are discussing refinancing in terms of finding extra money in your monthly budget, the focus here is on lowering your monthly mortgage payment. However, it's important to recognize when the change

might be too low to make the refinancing worthwhile. Refinancing might end up costing you more than standing pat if you do not factor in your closing costs and calculate your break-even point. You can generally expect to pay between $3,000 and $5,000 in closing costs/bank fees, so it may take many months at the lower mortgage payment amount before you recoup the upfront costs. Don't assume you can avoid these fees by taking a "no-cost" refinance—refinancing options that impose no upfront closing costs build those costs into the interest rate or principal balance.

3. *How will your loan term change?* If you are trying to reduce your monthly payment, it's unlikely that you will be able to shorten your loan term. If you are more than thirty years away from retirement, taking on a thirty-year refinance is not a problem. But if you are in your forties, fifties, or older, resetting the mortgage clock to thirty years when you hope to retire sooner than that can be too steep a price to pay for a lower monthly mortgage payment.

Consolidate Your Debt

In addition to your mortgage, the two types of debt that are most likely to cause you financial stress are credit card debt and student loan debt. Both of these debt types can be consolidated in order to reduce your monthly bills. We will discuss student loan consolidation in the second half of this section. Let's start by talking about what you can expect from credit card debt consolidation.

CREDIT CARD CONSOLIDATION

There are two ways to consolidate your credit card debt so that you can potentially lower your monthly payment: a personal consolidation loan or a debt management plan. Let's look at each of these options in turn:

A Personal Consolidation Loan

Both traditional banks and online lenders (including peer-to-peer lenders) offer plenty of personal loan options. When you qualify for a fixed-rate personal loan, you can use the proceeds to pay off your credit card debt and then pay a single monthly payment to your lender. These loans are unsecured, which means they are not supported by any type of collateral. Because of that, your interest rate with a personal consolidation loan depends greatly on your credit score.

Plenty of lenders out there offer personal loans you can use for debt consolidation, but you need to choose your lender wisely. Here are some questions you need to ask yourself before taking a personal loan to consolidate your credit card debt:

- *What rate do you qualify for?* According to the credit-counseling site Consolidated Credit (www.consolidatedcredit.org), you should never consolidate through a personal loan for an interest rate higher than 10 percent. Ideally, you should aim for a rate of 5 percent. If your interest rate is higher than 10 percent, too much of your monthly payments will be eaten up by interest. While this may offer you a smaller monthly payment, giving you some breathing room, your debt repayment plan will ultimately take longer and be much more expensive. If you cannot consolidate for a rate lower than 10 percent, then a personal loan may not be the right choice for you.
- *What is your loan term?* You want a repayment term that is long enough to lower your monthly payment but not so long that you end up spending more in interest over the life of the loan. Terms longer than five years tend to be detrimental to borrowers.
- *What will your monthly payment be?* Consolidating your debts into one loan does not necessarily guarantee a lower monthly payment.

Before taking out a personal loan, determine what the monthly payment will be and if it will help your monthly cash flow.

Beware of Using a Home Equity Loan to Consolidate Debt

Some borrowers may be tempted to take out a home equity loan to pay off their credit card (or other) debt. Often the loan terms for a home equity loan are more favorable, and the interest on a home equity loan is tax deductible.

But using your home equity loan to pay off your credit card debt can be very risky. If you are unable to get your credit card spending under control, you will find yourself in the same debt trap you were in before—except now you have used up the equity in your home. Additionally, you are trading unsecured debt (credit card) for secured debt (your home), which means that defaulting on your home equity loan could mean the bank forecloses on your home.

A Debt Management Plan

With this option, you can work with a credit-counseling agency to determine a workable payment plan. The agency then negotiates with your creditors to reduce or eliminate the interest charges applied to your debt.

A debt management plan tends to be the best choice for borrowers with sub-par credit scores. If you qualify for a debt management plan, you can generally expect to see between 30 percent and 50 percent reduction in your monthly payments and an interest rate reduced to below 10 percent. However, many borrowers will see their credit take a hit if they sign up for a debt management plan.

It's also important to remember that not all credit-counseling agencies are created equal. Here are the questions you need to ask before drawing up a debt management plan with a credit-counseling agency:

- *Does the agency charge a fee for information, or an upfront fee?* Some credit-counseling agencies are scams designed to prey on borrowers' desperation. If the agency you are in touch with does not provide free information about itself or its debt reduction process, consider that a red flag. Reputable credit-counseling agencies will not ask you for an upfront payment before they make a plan with you or before paying your creditors. The fees you pay should be part of your debt management plan, not a fee you pay beforehand.

- *What services does the agency offer?* Organizations that offer a range of services, including budgeting help and debt management classes in addition to debt management plans, are more likely to serve your best interests. Agencies that only offer debt management plans might overlook options that would work better for you.
- *How will this plan affect my credit?* Getting into a debt management plan can affect your credit score and limit your ability to acquire new credit while you are enrolled. This is not necessarily a reason to skip a plan that will help you reduce your monthly payments and improve your money behavior. However, it is an issue that you need to understand clearly and fully before signing on the dotted line.

STUDENT LOAN CONSOLIDATION

Student loans now account for $1.3 trillion in debt, making them the second biggest source of personal debt after mortgages. Because of this, many new banks and other types of lenders have been popping up to fill the very real need for student loan refinancing.

Student Loan Refinancing Comparison Tools

Finding a reputable lender can be a stressful endeavor for borrowers, since private student loan refinancing is still relatively new. The following tools offer a marketplace for student loan options. The benefit of using these tools is that you can quickly compare real offers from multiple lenders. Such marketplaces have the widest eligibility criteria, and you can compare rates before finishing the application process.

Consolidation versus Refinancing

The terms "refinance" and "consolidate" are sometimes used interchangeably when discussing student loans, but there are important differences between federal student loan consolidation and student loan refinancing.

With federal student loan consolidation, borrowers may consolidate multiple federal student loans into a single loan with a single repayment schedule. This kind of consolidation is only available for federal loans. You may not consolidate a private loan under federal student loan consolidation. Federal student loan consolidation does not usually save the borrower any money, since the borrower is charged the weighted average interest rate of all the loans being combined. However, consolidation can switch out a variable-rate loan for a fixed-rate loan, and it may lower monthly payments. The main reason to consider a federal student loan consolidation is to maintain the benefits available to federal borrowers, such as Public Service Loan Forgiveness, income-driven repayment plans, and deferral and forbearance options.

Private student loan refinancing allows a borrower to apply for a new loan that is used to pay off one or more existing loans. This is similar to consolidation, except that you may refinance both federal and private student loans, and you can potentially improve your interest rate and/or your monthly payment through private student loan refinancing. Refinancing federal student loans does mean you are no longer eligible for the federal benefits.

Credible

Dubbed the "Kayak.com for student loans," Credible (www.credible .com) offers a marketplace of student lenders for borrowers looking to refinance. Credible's unique dashboard allows for side-by-side comparison of refinanced loans, which you can then sort by and compare by annual percentage rate (APR), monthly payment, or total repayment amount. Borrowers must have more than $7,500 in federal or private student loans that are not currently in forbearance or deferment. Borrowers with a credit score lower than 680 will likely require a cosigner. Credible's site lets you know immediately if the interest rate offered to you is competitive, which will help you determine if you are a good candidate for refinancing. You will pay no fees to Credible for using their service.

LendEDU

Signing up with LendEDU (www.lendedu.com) allows you to compare rates for refinancing your student loan with up to nine different lenders. This gives you one-stop shopping when you decide to refinance. By using LendEDU, borrowers only need to enter a single lender application, and there are no hard credit pulls—so shopping around via LendEDU does not affect your credit score. Like Credible, borrowers pay no fees to LendEDU for using their services. LendEDU also offers many different video courses and guides to help borrowers make the best decisions for their money.

Use the Extra Money in Your Budget Wisely

No matter which method you choose for building some breathing room into your budget, you do need to be careful to use the extra money wisely. If you are prone to spending everything in your account, take the time to set up an automatic transfer of that extra money into your savings account. The cash will be there when you need it, relieving your scarcity-induced stress—but you will be protecting the money from your own temptation to spend it.

Chapter Ten Takeaways

1. Since living with the scarcity mindset can make it nearly impossible to improve your financial decisions, it is important to find actionable, realistic, and measurable methods for increasing your monthly cash flow.

2. Adjusting the withholding allowances on your W-4 form at work is a legal, quick, and painless way to increase your take-home pay with every paycheck.

3. Many of your monthly bills can be negotiated down with a few phone calls.

4. Unused subscriptions account for $14.3 billion in annual spending, according to a 2013 study. Paying closer attention to your account statements and canceling unused services can make a big difference in your monthly outlay.

5. Refinancing your mortgage may be a savvy way to reduce your mortgage payment, but you need to be aware of the potential downsides to your refinance.

6. Consolidating credit card debt through a personal consolidation loan or a debt management plan can potentially lower your monthly payments.

7. Refinancing your student loans through a private lender can give you some relief from high student loan payments, although you may also lose out on some federal student loan benefits if you refinance.

CHAPTER ELEVEN

Budgeting with Your Psychology in Mind

WHAT YOU'LL LEARN IN THIS CHAPTER

- Creating and adhering to a budget is a vital aspect of ending your financial stress. Following a budget will put you in control of your money.
- There are ways to create a budget that will fit within your personal preferences and psychology, but there is no getting around the need to periodically work on your finances.

Creating a budget is one of those tasks that people tend to avoid—like cleaning out the garage or undergoing dental surgery. Who can blame them? Crafting and adhering to a budget can sound like a combination of deprivation and work, and it can feel as though the stress of living without a budget is preferable to the stress of budgeting. Frankly, a root canal may sound less painful than the prospect of having to plan for and keep track of your spending.

Unfortunately, there is no getting around having to budget. Not even having a vast fortune at your disposal would insulate you from the need to budget, since you would still need to know where your huge amounts of money go.

Budgeting doesn't have to be painful. Creating your budget is about having the freedom to choose where your money goes, which can feel incredibly liberating. However, I understand that if you are budget-phobic, my saying this is not going to make you feel any more enthused about budgeting your money.

The good news is that there are multiple ways to productively budget your money, and it is possible to find a budgeting method that works for you. Let's start by talking about the basics of budgeting before we explore some of the ways you can create a budget that won't feel like pulling teeth.

Since understanding your income and outflow is the basis of all budgeting, you will want to complete the exercises that follow in the Budget Basics section no matter which budgeting option you ultimately choose. Though filling out these worksheets may take some work that will go against your psychological preferences, you only have to do these exercises when you initially create your budget. It is far more important to work within your psychological preferences when *adhering* to your budget, since that is where the rubber meets the road.

Budget Basics

A budget tracks two things: where your money comes from and where it goes. It is then up to you to institute the one essential budgeting action: spend less than you earn. Spending less does not have to be difficult, since we all have expenses that we can easily do without or can modify to be less expensive. However, until you know exactly what you're bringing in and where it's going, it can be almost impossible to figure out where to cut your spending. So to start the budgeting process, you must determine your income and your expenditures.

TRACKING YOUR INCOME

Tracking your income will generally be the easiest part of creating your budget. Unless you have irregular or variable income, it's pretty simple to look through your pay stubs in order to find out exactly how much you are bringing in each month.

However, you should also include any other sources of income that you may not usually think of as such—these include alimony, child support, rental income, disability checks, and dividends from stocks. To start, gather all of your income records for the past month (or year, for any income you receive irregularly), and start recording them in Worksheet 11-1: Tracking Your Income (courtesy of Tere Stouffer). You will be recording your net income—that is, the amount of money you see from each check after taxes, 401(k) contributions, union dues, or any other automatic withdrawals are removed.

For this worksheet, you will record your net income based on how often you are paid:

- Weekly
- Biweekly
- Semimonthly—this is when you always receive two paychecks per month, even in months with five weeks. For instance, you might be paid on the first and fifteenth of every month.
- Monthly—this money might come in the form of paycheck, disability check, alimony payment, rental income, and so forth.
- Quarterly—most likely this will include quarterly dividends from any stocks you own.
- Semiannually—you may receive some non-work-related income payments semiannually.
- Annually—you can include any bonuses that you know you will receive each year. If your bonuses are dependent on either your personal performance or your company's performance, then do not include them in your income calculations, as you cannot count on them.

Worksheet 11-1: Tracking Your Income

SOURCE OF INCOME	AMOUNT	MULTIPLY BY	ANNUAL AMOUNT
Weekly paycheck	_____	52	_____
Biweekly paycheck	_____	26	_____
Semimonthly paycheck	_____	24	_____
Monthly paycheck	_____	12	_____
Alimony	_____	12	_____
Child support	_____	12	_____
Disability check	_____	12	_____
Rental income	_____	12	_____
Quarterly payment	_____	4	_____
Semiannual payment	_____	2	_____
Annual payment	_____	1	_____
Total	$ _____		$_____

Now that you have your annual income total, you're ready to figure out how you spend that money.

TRACKING YOUR EXPENDITURES

Most people can count the number of their income sources on one hand—but that's certainly not the case with expenditures. There are an infinite number of ways you can spend your money, and the part of budgeting that usually has the budget-averse breaking out in hives is the idea of having to keep track of every one of those expenditures.

Luckily, in our modern world of online banking and debit and credit cards, this kind of tracking is not nearly as labor-intensive as it might sound. Take some time to log onto your bank and credit card website (or, gather together your bank and credit card statements, as well as your check register, if you have stuck with the paper-based system), and use the information to fill out Worksheet 11-2: Tracking Your Expenditures. Once you have completed that worksheet, you'll have an idea of your spending habits. From there, you can hone your understanding of where your money goes.

If you're new to budgeting, this might feel a little odd, since some of your expenditures are going to be irregular, such as the repair you needed to do on your car last spring, your spouse's dental surgery, or the amount you spent on a vacation. That's okay. To create a profile of your expenditures, gather the information on your spending over the past year to get an idea of what a typical year looks like. This exercise will help you to build room in your budget for your irregular expenditures, although they may change from year to year.

Worksheet 11-2: Tracking Your Expenditures

WEEKLY SPENDING	AMOUNT	MULTIPLY BY	ANNUAL AMOUNT
Groceries and household items (includes toiletries and cleaning supplies)		52	
Entertainment		52	
Dining out, including coffee and lunch		52	
Laundry/dry cleaning		52	
Gas/tolls/parking		52	
Public transportation		52	
Church/charitable contributions		52	
Postage and office supplies		52	
Walk-around money (include whatever cash you regularly carry for random weekly expenses)		52	
MONTHLY SPENDING	AMOUNT	MULTIPLY BY	ANNUAL AMOUNT
Mortgage/rent		12	
Car payment/lease		12	
Electric bill (average)		12	
Gas bill (average)		12	

	AMOUNT	MULTIPLY BY	ANNUAL AMOUNT
Water bill		12	
Sewer bill		12	
Trash pickup bill		12	
Cable/Internet/satellite bill		12	
Telephone bill		12	
Cell phone bill		12	
Bank charges (maintenance and debit card fees)		12	
Personal care (haircuts, manicures, etc.)		12	
Home equity loan		12	
Other loan		12	
Credit card bill (if you have more than one, total all payments together here)		12	
Child support		12	
Alimony		12	
Clothing		12	
Medical expenses (include copays and prescriptions)		12	
Memberships (gyms, professional organizations, religious institutions, etc.)		12	
QUARTERLY EXPENSES	**AMOUNT**	**MULTIPLY BY**	**ANNUAL AMOUNT**
Car maintenance		4	
Home maintenance		4	
Tuition (if you pay your child's college tuition more or less often than quarterly, simply multiply the amount of your payment by the number of payments you make in a year)		4	
Non-holiday gifts (include birthday, wedding, and baby gifts in this category)		4	
SEMIANNUAL EXPENSES	**AMOUNT**	**MULTIPLY BY**	**ANNUAL AMOUNT**
Auto insurance		2	
Property taxes		2	

ANNUAL EXPENSES	AMOUNT	MULTIPLY BY	ANNUAL AMOUNT
Homeowner's or renter's insurance	_____	12	_____
Vehicle registration and excise tax	_____	12	_____
Car repair	_____	12	_____
Home repair	_____	12	_____
Holiday gifts	_____	12	_____
Vacation	_____	12	_____
OTHER EXPENSES	AMOUNT	MULTIPLY BY	ANNUAL AMOUNT
	_____	_____	_____
	_____	_____	_____
	_____	_____	_____
Total	$_____		$_____

If you are living within your means, then your total expenditures amount will be lower than your total income amount. If you are either spending every penny that comes in or spending more than you make, then you will need to find some ways to reduce your expenditures. Even if you are already spending less than you earn, look at the amount left over at the end of each month. Ask yourself if you are saving enough for your goals. If not, reducing expenditures can help you reach your goals.

TAKING ANOTHER LOOK AT EXPENSES

Once you have calculated your intake and outflow, you can start looking for ways to reduce your expenses. Worksheet 11-3: Reworking Your Expenses is designed to help you do this. This worksheet will help you think about ways you can change your expenses and figure out how much money those changes will save you.

Remember that you do not need to make changes to every expense—or even most of them. The point is to make the most judicious cuts possible so that you can find extra money in your budget without affecting your priorities.

Though determining how to rework your expenses is all presented to you in a single neat table, this is by no means a quick process. It can take some time to implement your plans for lowering your expenses, so give yourself some time to work on your action plan (your "Ways to Reduce" from Worksheet 11-3). If your plan involves major shifts (like selling a house or a car), then you can expect this process to span several weeks—or even months. Even if your ways to reduce expenses are more modest, it's okay to pace yourself on the negotiations, contract changes, and other aspects of your plans that require you to do more than just change your habits. The most important thing is that you know what your expenses are and you have a plan in place for reducing them.

Worksheet 11-3: Reworking Your Expenses

EXPENSE	CURRENT AMOUNT	WAYS TO REDUCE	NEW AMOUNT
Mortgage/rent	_____	_____	_____
Car payment/lease	_____	_____	_____
Groceries and household items	_____	_____	_____
Entertainment	_____	_____	_____
Dining out	_____	_____	_____
Walk-around money (include whatever cash you regularly carry for random weekly expenses)	_____	_____	_____
Public transportation	_____	_____	_____
Electric bill	_____	_____	_____
Gas bill	_____	_____	_____
Water bill	_____	_____	_____
Trash pickup bill	_____	_____	_____
Cable/Internet/satellite bill	_____	_____	_____
Telephone bill	_____	_____	_____
Cell phone bill	_____	_____	_____
Credit card/loan payments	_____	_____	_____

Personal care (haircuts, etc.)	_____	_____	_____
Health/dental insurance	_____	_____	_____
Subscriptions	_____	_____	_____
Memberships	_____	_____	_____
Property taxes	_____	_____	_____
Homeowner's or renter's insurance	_____	_____	_____
Car insurance	_____	_____	_____
Miscellaneous	_____	_____	_____
Totals	Current Spending $_____		Amount Saved $_____

Now that you have a basic understanding of your annual income, your annual expenditures, and ways that you can reduce those expenditures, you are in the right place to create an ongoing budget for yourself that will fit within your psychological makeup.

Letting Something Else Track for You

Many would-be budgeters are capable of making great decisions with their money, as long as they don't have to track their spending themselves. For these people, having the information about how they spend their money is sufficient for them to stick to their budget. If this sounds like you, then you are a good candidate for personal finance software.

Here's how such software works: You set up an account with a budgeting software program, and then you connect all your banking, credit cards, and other financial accounts to the program so that it can track your expenses for you. After your initial setup, all you need to do is regularly log in to see how you are spending your money. The following five programs have all been proven to help beginning budgeters get a solid handle on their finances.

Security and Web-Based Budgeting Software

Many people worry about the security of their financial information when considering the use of a web-based budgeting software program. While I would never say that concern is unwarranted—hardly a few months go by without a story of a major retailer getting hacked—individuals who avoid budgeting software for this reason are not calculating their risks rationally. Personal finance software companies take security very seriously, and they do everything in their power to protect their users' information. The risk of a security breach is very low, and there is generally some sort of recourse guaranteed for users who do suffer a loss because of hacking. On the other hand, the risk of wasting your money by not tracking your expenses is pretty much assured. So unless you can force yourself to track expenses with paper and pencil, signing up for budgeting software is less financially risky than not doing so.

MINT (WWW.MINT.COM)

Founded in 2006, Mint is the original free web-based personal finance tracker. When you sign up with Mint, you provide the program with all your financial accounts, including bank accounts, investments, retirement funds, credit cards, 529 plan accounts, and the like. Mint allows you to see all your financial information in a single dashboard, which also calculates your net worth.

Using Mint, you can get into the nitty-gritty details of your finances. Mint tracks your transactions and automatically assigns an income or expense category for each one. It also assigns a default budget to each category of expenses, although you can create your own monthly budget, as well. The default mode is a nice way to start budgeting if you've never done so. You can see your financial progress using the trends function, which creates graphs and charts of your finances to help you understand where your money goes. Mint also helps you create goals—both savings and debt reduction—and tracks your progress.

Mint is entirely free, but there are affiliate offers on the site. These offers are optional and very easy to ignore.

MVELOPES (WWW.MVELOPES.COM)

Mvelopes is personal finance software that offers a twenty-first-century method for following the envelope-budgeting method, wherein budgeters set cash aside for different categories of spending. This online tool has both Android and iPhone versions that allow you to keep track of your spending on the go.

When you sign up with Mvelopes, you link up to four bank accounts (including checking accounts, credit card accounts, and PayPal accounts, among others) and create up to twenty-five spending "envelopes" to manage your spending. The program automatically tracks your transactions, which you then assign to the correct spending envelope. The amount of your transaction is subtracted from the money in that envelope. You may also manually track cash transactions.

One of the unique features of Mvelopes is how it handles credit card purchases. When a user makes a purchase using a credit card, the program removes the transaction amount from the spending envelope and places it in a special envelope to pay off the credit card. When your credit card bill arrives, the amount due is already set aside in the envelope, so you will be able to pay off your bill in full.

The basic Mvelopes program is free. The Premier version costs $95 per year and offers unlimited banks accounts and spending envelopes, as well as integrated premium video content and live chat support.

PERSONAL CAPITAL (WWW.PERSONALCAPITAL.COM)

One way to describe Personal Capital's budgeting software is as an "account aggregator." This program allows you to track and understand every penny in all your financial accounts. Once you link up all your various accounts, including your bank accounts, investments, mortgage, credit cards, and any other accounts, Personal Capital summarizes your finances and even offers you basic investment guidance.

Personal Capital also tracks investments; it offers a more comprehensive (and free!) service than its competitor, Mint. The program generates graphs and charts to help you better understand your financial picture, including the following categories:

- Net Worth
- Account Balances
- Income Reports
- Spending Reports
- Asset Allocation
- Investment Returns
- Projected Investment Fees

Basic budgeting is also a snap with this program, as the interface gives you an understanding of all your spending and account balances and allows you to categorize your spending by date, merchant, and type of expense. The associated mobile app for iPhone and Android allows you to keep track of your budget even when you're not at your computer.

QUICKEN (WWW.QUICKEN.COM/PRODUCTS)

First introduced back in 1983, Quicken is the great-granddaddy of personal finance software. The current version, Quicken 2017, was released in late 2016 and will be the final update by Intuit, since the company sold Quicken to a private equity firm.

For many people, Quicken's biggest selling point is that it is a software program you install on the hard drive of your computer, meaning all of your sensitive financial information is also stored there—making it secure from any potential hackers who are gunning for online personal finance programs. (This means you cannot access Quicken when you're on the go.)

In addition, because Quicken offers a great deal of customization and control, you can make the program work for your specific circumstances. The newest version of this software allows users to automatically track and pay bills.

Quicken is also well-known for its sunset provision that stops online features and formatted files from working after a certain time, which means users have to buy a new license to continue using the software. Often, these updates also include a new interface, meaning users have to relearn the program after each update.

The program costs between $40 and $110, depending upon which software package you purchase.

YNAB (WWW.YOUNEEDABUDGET.COM)

You Need a Budget (YNAB) is an online budgeting program also based on the envelope method. The program guides you through the process of budgeting, setting goals and sticking to them, and reconciling accounts.

The philosophy behind YNAB is built on four basic rules that will help users live within their means:

1. Give Every Dollar a Job—All money you receive is assigned to a specific budget category.

2. Embrace Your True Expenses—Understand your irregular expenses.

3. Roll with the Punches—You can strategically rearrange budget categories if your spending doesn't exactly align with your plans.

4. Age Your Money—You can end the paycheck-to-paycheck cycle by building a buffer of one month's cash in hand.

YNAB believes that in order to successfully budget, you need to be hands-on with your money. Until the most recent version was released in December 2015, users had to manually enter all transactions— although the program and its companion apps for iPhone, iPad, and Android devices made this very easy to do. This also means that YNAB is one of the few programs that easily allows users to track cash spending.

The updated program automatically imports transactions, but it is up to the user to assign each transaction to its appropriate budget category. You may use manual entry if you prefer, or a combination of automatic and manual.

In addition to the program, signing up for YNAB gets you access to financial literacy classes, tutorials, a community of YNAB users, blog posts, and budgeting tools and tricks.

At $50 for a twelve-month subscription, YNAB is not the cheapest personal finance program around, but you get a generous thirty-four-day free trial before you commit.

If You Don't Want to Track Your Expenses at All

Certified Financial Planner Roger P. Whitney works in finance, but he doesn't have time to manage the minutiae necessary to follow a monthly budget. Rather than work as his own part-time bookkeeper, he created a system that he calls the Cash Flow Bucket System—a system you can use, too. This system allows you to stick to a budget and set money aside into savings without having to keep track of your expenditures. According to Whitney's website The Retirement Answer Man (RogerWhitney .com), there are four steps to creating this budgeting system:

STEP 1: DETERMINE YOUR MONTHLY LIFESTYLE BUDGET

Whitney defines your monthly lifestyle budget as the amount of money you need each month to maintain your lifestyle—while still living within your means. To determine your monthly lifestyle budget, you will need to know your monthly income, your fixed monthly expenses, and your variable monthly expenses. You can calculate your monthly numbers by using the annual income and expenses that you calculated using the Worksheets in this chapter, and then divide those totals by twelve.

(When creating your Cash Flow Bucket System, you need to tread carefully with your monthly income calculations if you included annual bonuses or other irregular income in your annual income calculation. If you did include those income sources, just use the monthly income that you know you can count on.)

Annual Income _____ / 12 = _____ Monthly Income
Annual Expenses _____ / 12 = _____ Monthly Expenses

Theoretically, your monthly expenses should be lower than your monthly income. If they are not, keep working on ways to reduce your expenses. Use Worksheet 11-3 to help you with this task. If you determine that your expenses are below your income, then you can set your expense amount as being your monthly lifestyle budget amount.

STEP 2: SET UP AN INCOME ACCOUNT

With this step, you will open a separate savings or checking account to receive all your income. You will deposit any and all cash inflows to that account.

STEP 3: ESTABLISH A MONTHLY TRANSFER

On the first of each month, you will transfer your monthly lifestyle budget amount from your income account to your spending account. You will spend that money each month without having to worry about tracking your spending.

Your spending account will be nearly depleted by the end of the month, but if you correctly calculated your monthly lifestyle budget, the money should last until the first of the following month. If you are running short prior to the end of the month, you will need to look at your expenses to see where your calculation went wrong or where your spending was too high. You can also decide to move more money from your income account to your spending account or go on a financial fast (that is, make no purchases until the next month begins) to make it to the next month.

STEP 4: ADJUST AND DECIDE

Finally, Whitney suggests you review your Cash Flow Bucket System every three months. During your quarterly review, look back to see if and how often you had to transfer additional funds from your income account to your spending account. If this was a consistent problem, you can work on reducing your expenses again or, if you made a mistake initially, recalculate your monthly lifestyle budget amount. In addition, the quarterly review will give you an opportunity to see if there is excess cash built up in your income account—which there will be if you have not had to make additional transfers each month. You can take this time to decide where your excess money will go to help you reach your financial goals.

If You Want to (Productively) Ignore Your Money

If thinking about your money is just one more thing you're not going to get to on your ever-growing to-do list, then automatic savings and budgeting apps might be the solution to your budgeting woes. These apps each have a different approach to automating your finances, but they all allow reluctant budgeters the opportunity to continue to ignore their money, but in a productive fashion.

DIGIT (DIGIT.CO)

This completely free program syncs with your bank accounts and analyzes your cash flow. Every two to three days, it will determine an amount of money (between $5 and $50) that is safe to transfer into an FDIC-insured Digit deposit account. Digit is so confident in its safe-to-withdraw algorithms that it offers to pay overdraft fees if a transfer leaves you overdrawn. You can request money from your Digit account anytime, and you will generally receive it the next business day.

Digit communicates with you via text message, and you must sign up online, as it is technically not an app. You will receive a text message once per day with your current bank balance. You also have the option to receive more detailed text check-ins, which allow you to see recent debits. This can give you a no-effort daily snapshot of your finances.

The big downside to Digit is that you will earn no interest on your deposit account, since the interest earned in those accounts pays for the program's operating costs. This is how the program remains completely free.

LEVEL MONEY (WWW.LEVELMONEY.COM)

The Level Money app syncs with your bank account and determines how much will be left in that account after automatically deducting upcoming bills, recent purchases, and your savings goals. It then gives you an estimate of the amount of money that's safe for you to spend over the next day, week, and month.

In addition, the app also offers an Insights section that allows you to track a certain category of spending. For instance, you might create a "coffee" category and have the app track all your spending in your favorite café. The app will then show you how much you have spent on coffee over the past month, and will calculate your average monthly coffee expenses if you continue caffeinating at the same rate, as well as your projected annual amount spent on coffee.

Level Money will let you know if you are getting too close to over-spending your account, but it is still entirely up to you to keep from blowing through all your money. Level Money is completely free of fees.

PENNIES (WWW.GETPENNIES.COM)

This very intuitive iPhone app helps even the most absent-minded spenders stay on budget. Pennies allows you to set a number of budgets (such as monthly fun money, weekly food spending, and the like) with a start date, length of budget term, and the amount available to spend. Each time you make a purchase, you enter the amount into Pennies, which will show you the number of dollars and days remaining in that budget.

The app uses colors to help you gauge the health of your budget—a red background shows you that your money is quickly dwindling, while green and blue lets you know you are cleared for additional purchases. If you forget to log purchases, you'll get an occasional reminder from the app to go back to tracking.

Pennies does not sync with your financial institutions and only tracks a single source of money at a time, which can make things a little difficult for anyone with multiple bank accounts or payment methods. Pennies costs $2.99 in the iTunes store. There are no other fees.

RIZE (WWW.RIZEUP.IO)

Rize is a brand-new entry in the world of automatic savings, and it is set up to help you pay yourself first. After you receive a paycheck, Rize automatically moves money from your checking account to your Rize account. Each time Rize moves money into that account, the app sends you a notification via text or e-mail with an update on your savings progress.

The program also helps you choose a savings amount that fits with your age, income, and location, and it suggests smart financial goals that match your situation—although you can always create your own custom goals. Rize also helps users by suggesting increases to the amount saved each month as your circumstances change.

To make sure Rize does not overdraw your checking account, the program notifies you of the transfer a few days before it happens, giving you time to pause the transaction. Rize also automatically double-checks the balance in your checking account before the transfer to make sure you have sufficient funds.

Your Rize account is a savings account that earns 0.30 percent APY (annual percentage yield) interest, although rates are subject to change. As a savings account, Rize also offers SIPC insurance protection up to $250,000, similar to FDIC insurance of the same amount in a traditional bank. You may withdraw money from your Rize account at any time.

By far the most unusual aspect of Rize is how it handles fees. There is no set monthly fee for the program, but Rize asks users to contribute a small amount of the money you save each month—the exact amount is up to the user.

Budgeting Keeps Your Relationship with Money Healthy

I suspect some of my readers may have reached this point in the chapter feeling a little disappointed. I promised you several methods for creating a budget that would fit within your psychology, rather than against it—and yet all of the options I listed still require you to do some work.

Unfortunately, there is no magic trick that will make budgeting effortless. That's because budgeting is an active choice that you have to make in order to keep your relationship with money healthy. Just as your marriage, friendships, and family relationships cannot simply coast along without effort on your part, your budget requires you to put in regular effort to keep your relationship with money from becoming toxic.

Certified Financial Planner Mindy Crary explains in *Forbes* that "you can't enjoy a good relationship with money unless you're willing to [honor the relationship]."

Specifically, Crary suggests that you honor your relationship with money by paying attention to it, just as you would your spouse: "You would never roll your eyes and tell [your spouse], 'I'll deal with you later!'" In addition, making time for and prioritizing your relationship with money are both just as important as doing so for your personal relationships. Honoring your money in this way is what will make your budgeting successful, no matter which budgeting method you choose to follow.

Though it may seem overwhelming or unpleasant to think about maintaining your budget, remember that budgeting is similar to the relationship work you do to maintain your marriage or your friendships. When you take care of your loved ones, they are there to take care of you.

If you take good care of your money, it can take better care of you, too.

Chapter Eleven Takeaways

1. Budgeting starts with understanding your income and outflow. Once you have that information, you are able to be more intentional in how you use your money.

2. Would-be budgeters who do not want to personally track their spending can use personal finance software to capture that information for them.

3. Those who do not want to do any expense tracking can create a Cash Flow Bucket System, wherein the only money in their account is the amount necessary to fulfill their monthly financial needs.

4. Individuals who would prefer to completely ignore their money can do so productively by using automatic savings and budgeting apps.

5. No matter which budget option you choose, you will have to put in some work on maintaining your budget.

CHAPTER TWELVE

Increase Your Level of Self-Discipline

WHAT YOU'LL LEARN IN THIS CHAPTER

- Improving your self-discipline is a necessary component to ending financial stress.
- Your locus of control determines whether you feel in control of life, or controlled by it. Shifting your locus of control so that you feel more powerful can help you improve your financial decisions.
- Financial self-efficacy describes how competent you feel in managing your money. Low self-efficacy is correlated with poor financial decisions, but you can raise your self-efficacy.
- Exercising willpower is mentally exhausting, which is why it can be so difficult to resist temptations in the moment.
- There are practical ways to improve willpower in order to keep temptations from ruining your hard work.

Prior to this chapter, we have talked about learning to work within your financial psychology so that you are not fighting your own nature in order to improve your finances. However, even if you create and follow a budget that fits your psychology and abilities to a T, you will still face spending temptations on a regular basis. Learning how to say, "Thanks, but no thanks" to such temptations can be one of the most difficult aspects of ending your financial stress, especially if you are dealing with the kind of scarcity mindset we discussed in Chapter 4.

The end of unnecessary spending is crucial if you want to end your financial stress. Trying to improve your finances without putting an end to impulsive spending is like trying to shovel the walk before it stops snowing. You are not going to make real headway.

The good news is that your level of self-discipline is not etched in stone, and it is possible for you to improve your ability to resist temptation. At the end of the chapter we will talk about practical methods for dealing with temptation in the moment. First, though, we will talk about the kinds of entrenched thought patterns that can act as willpower-sappers, before you're even tempted by the *once-in-a-lifetime!* sale prices.

Locus of Control

The term "locus of control" refers to how individuals see their ability to control the events in their lives. If you have an internal locus of control, you believe you have a great deal of power over your life. If your locus of control is external, on the other hand, you feel as though life happens to you and you have very little power to exert control over it.

For example, let's say Melissa has a big test for her economics course. She is very busy during the week of her test and doesn't hit the books as she intended. The test comes back with a big fat F on top.

Melissa has an internal locus of control, so she recognizes that she just didn't study enough for the exam. She feels pretty lousy about the grade, but she understands that she can do better on the next test as long as she prioritizes studying. When she aces the following exam, Melissa sees that success as evidence that she prepared well for the test, and she feels great about it.

Another student in the class, Teddy, has an external locus of control. Teddy flunks the same test that Melissa failed. He also feels terrible about the grade, but he decides that the test was too hard, the questions were bad, and the teacher was out to get him.

What's depressing for Teddy is that even if he aces an exam, he will not feel good about doing well on it. Instead of congratulating himself for doing a good job of studying, Teddy is more likely to believe the teacher was being too easy or that he was lucky. Since his locus of control is external, he is not able to feel proud of his accomplishments.

Studies have shown that individuals with an internal locus of control like Melissa are happier than their external locus counterparts like Teddy. This is because people with an internal locus of control believe that they can make their own lives better.

In addition, psychologists have theorized that the Melissas of the world are less likely to get into debt. That's because these go-getter types recognize that their finances are entirely within their control. As a result, they make proactive decisions about their money management. If they do end up in dire financial straits, individuals with an internal locus of control will recognize that they are responsible for the predicament and that they are therefore responsible for fixing the problem.

External locus of control types, on the other hand, may feel as though nothing they do matters much. Poor Teddy likely believes that it's impossible to beat the banks at their own game, that living with debt is how The Man keeps him down, and that any financial gains he experiences are attributable to luck.

Within the personal finance community, an excellent example of someone who clearly has an internal locus of control is author and motivational speaker Mary Hunt. She and her family racked up more than $100,000 in credit card debt over a decade. While many people in her position would have declared bankruptcy and started over, Mary and her family decided to pay off every penny of what they owed, which meant completely changing the family's lifestyle. It took the Hunt family thirteen years to pay it all off. To Mary, it was clear she had gotten herself into the mess, and it was therefore up to her to get back out of it.

YOUR CHILDHOOD SHAPES YOUR LOCUS OF CONTROL

If people with an internal and external locus of control were evenly distributed among socioeconomic classes, then we could surmise that your locus of control is simply part of your psychological makeup.

However, a 2014 study published by the American Psychological Association (APA) found that growing up poor can lead to a loss of one's sense of control when facing uncertainty—whether that uncertainty is economic or of any other stripe. Growing up wealthy, on the other hand, means that one tends to feel a greater sense of internal control when dealing with uncertain situations.

For instance, the APA study found that people who grew up without much money are more likely to take a small, immediate reward instead of a larger, later reward. Psychologists believe that learning to take something that is immediately offered is a protective and reactive behavior pattern, based on an external locus of control. In the context of a financially tumultuous childhood, this behavior pattern makes perfect sense. When you do not trust that the outside world will treat you well or fairly, then you are likely to grab what you can when you can.

Unfortunately, this kind of impulsiveness is part of what leads to higher debt and lower savings among those with an external locus of control. Waiting patiently for a larger, later reward is what saving money and investing are all about, after all.

To make matters worse for those who have an external locus of control, feeling as though you do not have control can also affect your sense of determination. One part of the APA study asked participants to recall a moment of financial uncertainty, and immediately afterward they were given an unsolvable puzzle. Those participants who had grown up poor gave up on the puzzle 25 percent sooner than those from wealthier backgrounds. This is a reactive behavior pattern that indicates an external locus of control—"The world is too tough and I just can't get ahead!"

Just imagine how many people have given up on their dreams at the first setback because of such reactive behavior patterns.

Shifting Your Locus of Control

If you developed an external locus of control from your childhood or other difficult financial situations in your life, all is not lost. It is possible to shift your locus of control if you engage in two scientifically proven thought exercises:

RECALL A TIME WHEN YOU FELT IN CONTROL

The authors of the APA study found that asking participants to recall situations when they were in control helped to ameliorate their feeling of not being in control of their lives. This quick thought exercise helps to shift your locus of control because it helps you to feel more confident in the moment.

If you tend to feel out of control when you are facing economic uncertainty, think of a time when you handled a problem in a way that you were proud of. The example you recall does not have to be financial in nature for this exercise to work. Remembering your feeling of control can help you maintain that sensation of control while facing uncertainty.

Such confidence can help you to do well in the new situation, which in turn brings you more confidence. Once you are in the habit of feeling confident and in control, you will have even more examples to call upon when things are uncertain.

TALK TO YOURSELF BY NAME

While each of us engages in self-talk—that inner conversation you hold with yourself and use to evaluate what you're doing as you do it—those with an external locus of control have a tendency to engage in negative self-talk. For instance, those with an external locus of control might think things like, *This is too much for me to handle* or *What's the use of even trying?*

The importance of changing your self-talk to be more positive is so widely known that it has become almost laughable. (Whenever I hear about the importance of positive self-talk I tend to think of Al Franken's ridiculous self-help guru character Stuart Smalley intoning, "I'm good enough, I'm smart enough, and doggone it, people like me!") It can be very difficult for people to change the tone of their inner monologues if they've been berating themselves for a lifetime. This can be particularly challenging if you feel like you're imitating Stuart Smalley anytime you try. But psychologist Ethan Kross has found that one simple word can make an enormous difference in your ability to psych yourself up rather than down: your name.

When you talk to yourself by name, rather than using I, the switch to third-person creates enough psychological distance that your brain enables you to practice more self-control. Kross writes in *Psychology Today*, "First name self-talk shifts the focus away from the self; it allows people to transcend their inherent ego-centrism. And that makes them as smart in thinking about themselves as they typically are about others."

By talking to yourself as if you were talking to a friend, you gain the benefits of both being interested but distant from the problem (as if it were happening to a friend), and of being psyched up by a proud friend.

This means that referring to yourself in the third person during self-talk can help you to feel more powerful, and gradually internalize your locus of control.

Self-Efficacy

Self-efficacy is a related concept to locus of control in that self-efficacy measures just how competent you feel in a particular area of expertise. For instance, Mark is a mechanic, which means he would feel very little stress if his car were to break down on vacation. Just give Mark some tools and some time, and he will likely be able to either fix or diagnose the problem. He has a high sense of self-efficacy when it comes to automotive issues.

On the other hand, Mark may break into a cold sweat at the idea of having to manage his money.

While people may have a sense of high self-efficacy in one area of their lives, they may feel out of their depth in another area. Having low self-efficacy means that you believe the task at hand is harder than it is, and you are more likely to be stressed by it and more likely to avoid the work.

Psychologists theorize that individuals with low financial self-efficacy are more likely to get into debt and stay there. The theory suggests that these individuals choose not to think about their financial decisions because they do not feel up to the task.

Money is an inescapable part of life in our society. You may not need to know about the mechanics of an internal combustion engine to drive a car, but you must know something about money if you hope to handle it well. When Mark chooses not to think about his financial decisions, he puts himself at risk for making poor money choices. In addition, because of his low financial self-efficacy, if Mark gets into debt or other financial trouble he might not see himself as being capable of tackling the problem or the behaviors that got him into trouble.

Research has also shown that general low self-efficacy—feeling incapable of handling issues in any area of one's life—is correlated with low self-esteem. That means the individuals who simply do not feel competent in their lives will look for other ways to give themselves a much-needed boost—like by going shopping.

SELF-EFFICACY AND COPING STRATEGIES

When you indulge in recreational shopping you are using a coping strategy for dealing with your feelings of helplessness. There is a reason why we call the artificial boost from shopping "retail therapy."

In fact, the psychology of addiction can help us understand why it is that we head to the mall (or to the donut shop or to the bar or to the casino) after a bad day at work. According to Dr. Lance Dodes of *Psychology Today*, "Every addictive act is preceded by a feeling of helplessness or powerlessness. Addictive behavior functions to repair this underlying feeling of helplessness." Helplessness is the result of low self-efficacy.

Many individuals adopt negative financial coping strategies in order to deal with their feelings of helplessness. This is why Mark might get so stressed over his Visa bill that he heads off to the nearest Best Buy and drops $200 on new video games. His sense of helplessness over the size of the bill is spurring him on to shop more, even though that is objectively the worst possible course of action he can take.

Improving Your Self-Efficacy

Like your locus of control, your sense of self-efficacy can be changed—and the strategies for shifting your locus of control will also have the effect of raising your sense of self-efficacy. However, researchers have found that there are additional antidotes to low financial self-efficacy that can help you feel more capable of taking care of your money:

CONTINUING FINANCIAL EDUCATION

Dr. William Lapp of EARN Research Institute, a nonprofit micro-savings provider, recently conducted a study on the effects of financial education on low-income workers. He found that a very basic education was not enough to increase self-efficacy in participants, but "increases in their financial knowledge *above and beyond baseline levels* further increased their financial self-efficacy, which in turn reduced their financial problems."

Reading this book is an excellent start toward improving your financial education, but making such education an intentional part of your life going forward will continue to increase your sense of financial self-efficacy. You will find suggestions for further reading at the end of this book.

USE SMALL WINS TO CHANGE YOUR SELF-TALK

As with your locus of control, a big component of improving your sense of financial self-efficacy lies in changing your self-talk. When Mark tells himself that he is just no good with money, the negative message affects his performance of money management.

Sports psychologist Dr. Jennifer Cumming has studied the effects of self-talk and guided imagery on sports performance. She has found that negative self-talk, coupled with imagining failure, worsened participants' performance; whereas positive self-talk and imagining success, improved participants' performance.

How do you go about changing your self-talk if it is a script you have been following your entire life? The secret lies in the power of small wins.

Dr. Teresa Amabile, the Edsel Bryant Ford Professor of Business Administration at Harvard Business School, has dubbed the feeling of making progress on meaningful work "the progress principle." She writes in the *Harvard Business Review* that "the more frequently people experience that sense of progress—even [with] a small win—the more likely they are to be creatively productive in the long run."

Feeling as though you are making progress on mastering your finances helps to boost your sense of financial self-efficacy, which then helps you to make even more progress. So small wins can help to start a snowball of greater progress, more positive self-talk, and higher self-efficacy.

How do you harness the power of small wins if you start by feeling completely helpless? Habit and behavior expert James Clear has found that you can start experiencing small wins by creating identity-based habits.

This strategy runs counter to the usual advice about setting goals, which recommends aiming for a large change in your life. Unfortunately, those large goals can feel impossible to achieve, and the first setback or mistake will often be enough to make us return to our old, entrenched habits.

Instead of adopting an all-or-nothing big-dream goal, Clear recommends that you decide what type of person you want to be and prove to yourself that you are that sort of person with small wins.

For instance, Mark might decide he wants to get out of debt. Instead of setting a big goal like I will pay off all my debt this year, Mark could decide to become the sort of person who sends an extra payment to his creditors each week, no matter how small. Those small wins will add up, so that he not only begins to self-identify as someone who is paying off his debt, but he will also feel more effective in money management.

The progress he makes will help him to rewrite his negative self-talk and improve his sense of financial self-efficacy.

Similarly, if you decide to become the sort of person who understands finance, you can set a small win of reading a book about money each quarter or reading one article from a financial magazine or website each week. The identity-based habits will help you to slowly become the person you want to identify as being, which is a more sustainable path to change than setting a big goal.

Dealing with Temptations in the Moment

In addition to the entrenched habits of thought that can make self-discipline and change very difficult, you must also deal with the sudden appearances of temptations. Pause for a moment to reflect on how you deal with those sorts of temptations.

While studies have found that there is a difference in the prefrontal cortex (the area of the brain associated with impulse control) between those people who have impulsive tendencies and those with high self-discipline, the basic building blocks of immediate self-discipline are learnable. Recent research into self-control has shown that the key to saying no to temptations is to avoid them.

Time magazine reported on this research in 2013, stating that highly self-disciplined individuals "tend to avoid creating situations in which their goals would conflict, and reported fewer instances of having to choose between short-term pleasure and long-term pain." That is, staying true to your long-term goals is less about finding the willpower to resist temptations, and more about setting up your life to avoid those temptations altogether.

What if you can't avoid such temptations? How do you muster the willpower to say no to the short-term pleasure that will have a long-term cost? To understand how to improve your willpower, you need to start with an understanding of what willpower is.

WHY WILLPOWER IS EXHAUSTING

Willpower is a type of self-regulation. When the donuts are passed around at the morning meeting, your willpower prompts you to pass the box along without taking a chocolate-glazed for yourself. It's also what prompts you to forgo favorite little luxuries when you are trying to save money. You are entirely in control over whether you eat the donut or spend the money, as no one will force you to do either one.

However, as anyone who has ever struggled with a New Year's resolution can attest, it can be much more difficult to regulate yourself than it should. Since no one is forcing you to take the donut, why does it sometimes feel as though you don't really have a choice in the matter?

According to journalist John Tierney, coauthor of the book *Willpower: Rediscovering the Greatest Human Strength*, self-regulatory behavior, which includes everything from exercising willpower to making decisions, exhausts us. The act of making a decision—whether it's one in line with your goals and requires willpower, or one that simply needs to be made—saps mental energy in a process known as "ego depletion." As that happens, we become weaker in the face of temptation and we experience things more intensely.

In 2011, Tierney described ego depletion to Audie Cornish of NPR:

Basically, it's that everything feels more intensely to you. Good things and bad things. You suddenly feel everything a little bit more intensely because your brain has lost some ability to regulate emotions, and so you therefore respond more strongly to everything.

This is related to the kind of tunnel focus brought on by the scarcity mindset that we talked about in Chapter 4. As we discussed in that chapter, it can be incredibly difficult to force yourself out of such a mindset—but there are several tricks you can use to help self-regulate in the moment, even while you are doing the more global work of shifting your locus of control and improving your financial self-efficacy.

Distract Yourself

In the late 1960s, psychologist Walter Mischel conducted research on willpower; this has come to be known as the "Stanford marshmallow experiment." In this experiment, Mischel gave four- and five-year-old children a marshmallow or other treat and told them they could have a second treat if they could hold off on eating the one in front of them for fifteen minutes. The children who were able to wait for the second marshmallow distracted themselves by hiding their eyes, singing songs, or pretending the marshmallow was a cloud.

Those little kids were onto something. People with excellent willpower often remove temptations from their path—such as a dieter's house with no ice cream or cookies in it—or they think of something else in order to ignore the temptation. Focusing your brain on something other than the temptation allows you the mental space you need to ignore it. If you find yourself tempted to spend money you can't afford, start to think instead about the reason you are trying to improve your financial situation. It will help motivate you to stay on track while giving your brain something other than the temptation to think about.

Have a Snack

It turns out your mother was right: You *do* think better after you've had something to eat. According to a 2007 study by Matthew T. Gailliot and Roy F. Baumeister, the ability to self-regulate depends in part on blood-glucose levels. This is part of the reason why you may feel more alert and able to power through your to-do list right after lunch as opposed to right beforehand. It's also why it's so hard to stick to a grocery list if you go shopping on an empty stomach. If you're feeling tempted by something you know you need to avoid, have a piece of fruit or another complex carbohydrate. It can help you get your will-power back on track.

Remember Your Motivation

Part of the reason why ego depletion often causes you to give in to temptation is because it can reduce your motivation.

Dr. Timothy Pychyl, in an article for *Psychology Today*, explains this loss of motivation as a sense that success is too far away: "Given that depleted self-regulatory strength may leave us feeling like we won't suc-ceed, 'we're too tired to try,' it may be that the reduced expectancy of success undermines our willingness to exert effort. It's not that we're so impaired that we can't respond. It's that we 'don't feel like it.'"

A great example of how motivation can change your ability to do something occurred on the day of the 2013 Boston Marathon bombing. On that day, many marathoners who had just finished a 26.2-mile race decided to run an additional 2 miles to Massachusetts General Hospital in order to donate blood—even though under normal circumstances they would have been too exhausted after the race to run another step. They found the physical strength and stamina after the tragedy to keep running and donate blood because their motivation was high.

It's easy to forget your motivation when you are trying to improve your money management skills since the goal can feel too large to make a dent. There are several ways you can keep your motivation front and center:

1. *Create an age-progressed picture of yourself:* Researchers have found that you will feel more connected to and protective of your future self if you can see what you will look like as an elderly man or woman. You can create such pictures at www.in20years.com.

2. *Post pictures of a financial goal:* Putting such images around your home, in your wallet, and on your computer will help keep your motivation on top of your mind.

3. *Imagine the worst-case scenario:* Think through your biggest financial fear and let yourself think about living through that possibility. Fear can be a powerful motivator.

4. *Change your passwords to represent a financial goal:* For instance, you might make your password the year your child will start college and the name of a preferred school—such as 2021OSU. It will keep your goal front-and-center, particularly if you are signing on to a retail shopping site.

Plan with Morning Guy in Mind

A 2013 UCLA study discovered that differences in how languages refer to future events can affect our behavior. For instance, English has a very distinct future tense. If we want to talk about tomorrow's weather, we say, "It will rain tomorrow." In languages with a less distinct future tense (such as German, for example), speakers say, "It rains tomorrow." That seemingly slight difference means that English speakers' brains encode the future as a time distinct from now, while German speakers do not.

Where this gets interesting is that speakers of languages with less linguistic distinction between the present and the future "save more, retire with more wealth, smoke less, practice safer sex, and are less obese."

That means we English speakers are at a distinct disadvantage. We already tend to see the future as somebody else's problem because of hyperbolic discounting—the cognitive bias that makes us prefer the instant, the immediate, and the now over the future. Because of hyperbolic discounting, we "discount" things that will happen far in the future as being less important than those things occurring right now.

Add in a language that codifies the differences between the present and the future, and we are very likely to give in to today's temptations and let our future selves deal with the consequences.

The comedian Jerry Seinfeld has a classic bit about this problem:

"I never get enough sleep. I stay up late at night, cause I'm Night Guy. Night Guy wants to stay up late.

"'What about getting up after five hours sleep?'

"Oh that's Morning Guy's problem. That's not my problem, I'm Night Guy. I stay up as late as I want.

"So you get up in the morning, you're exhausted, groggy. Oooh, I hate that Night Guy! See, Night Guy always screws Morning Guy. There's nothing Morning Guy can do."

In Seinfeld's humorous observation lies a possible solution to the problem of English's future tense and its effect on our self-discipline. Start thinking about what your Morning Guy would most like to "wake up to." For Seinfeld, that would mean going to bed at a decent hour. For someone hoping to improve her finances, that could mean setting money aside into an emergency fund, waiting to buy something until she could pay for it in cash, or increasing her contribution to her retirement account.

Taking the time to think through what your "Morning Guy" will want in the future makes it much easier to act in accordance with your goals in the present.

Chapter Twelve Takeaways

1. Improving self-discipline requires you to both root out entrenched negative thought patterns and deal constructively with temptations in the moment.

2. Shifting to an internal locus of control by remembering instances when you felt in control and by changing to third-person self-talk will help you feel as though you can make a difference in your life.

3. Learning more about finances and setting yourself up for small wins will improve your sense of financial self-efficacy.

4. The best way to resist temptation is to avoid it; distracting yourself, having a small snack, or keeping your motivation in the forefront of your mind will help you deal with immediate temptations that you cannot avoid.

5. Thinking through what you would want your future self to experience can help you make better financial decisions now.

CHAPTER THIRTEEN

Letting Go of Financial Resentment

WHAT YOU'LL LEARN IN THIS CHAPTER

- Financial resentment is the ongoing anger and disappointment we feel because of a real or perceived money-related injustice.
- Holding on to financial resentment can cause disordered and self-sabotaging financial behavior.
- You may feel resentment on a personal level or your resentment may be based upon larger issues, such as the economy as a whole. Both types of resentments are corrosive and damaging to your financial peace.
- Ending your resentful feelings is neither easy nor simple, but it is possible to let go of the anger you feel over past injustices.

Being treated unfairly is one of the most upsetting experiences that we all face. Living through such injustice angers us, and it settles in our psyche as resentment. When we resent others because of an injustice—whether it is a real injustice or an imagined one—we cannot help but feel anger, sadness, disappointment, and disgust that tends to strengthen rather than fade over time. The fact that resentment grows over time is one of the most insidious aspects of this corrosive emotion. Our upset feelings are retriggered every time we think about the original injustice, which adds fuel to resentment fire. According to Dr. Steven Stosny, writing for *Psychology Today*:

> Resentment is more of a mood than an emotional state, and the behaviors it motivates are more habit than choice. . . . The habitual nature of resentment means that it is never specific to one behavior—nobody resents just one thing—and that its content is rarely forgotten. Instead, each new incident of perceived unfairness automatically links onto previous ones, eventually forging a heavy chain. . . . The tremendous effort required to drag the chain of resentment through life makes us hyper-vigilant for possible ego offenses, lest they "sneak up" on us. In other words, the chain of resentment makes us look for things to resent.

Garden-variety resentment is a serious problem in any number of relationships and situations, but it is financial resentment that may be keeping you from ending your financial stress.

Financial resentment occurs when we cling to outrage over financial injustices, whether they are real or perceived. Though all resentment is corrosive, financial resentment can be a more dangerous version of the emotion, for three reasons:

1. *Money appears to be a simple matter of numbers*, making us vulnerable to the false belief that the injustices we feel over money are clear-cut and absolute. This is unlike the injustices we might feel over family favoritism, divorce, or other relationship issues, wherein it is possible for you to recognize that there are gray areas.

2. *Financial resentment tends to be a socially acceptable emotion*, which means that it can be used as an emotional screen for other resentments you feel. As Dr. Stosny points out, resentment rarely has a single cause. Your financial resentment likely stems from more than just the financial injustice you have suffered, but you are likely to feel less social pushback for your resentment if you can point to a financial cause. This is not to say that those who feel financial resentment do not have cause to be angry. However, carrying

resentment can fuel ugly or problematic behavior that seems much more socially justified if the resentment is financial in nature.

3. While all feelings of resentment might cause you to engage in self-destructive behavior, *financial resentment leaves you vulnerable to disordered and self-sabotaging money behavior.* For instance, those feeling financial resentment might spend money they can't afford in an attempt to right the injustice that caused their resentment.

There are two ways that financial resentment may manifest itself: as relationship-based resentment, and as resentment of larger economic problems. Both of these types of resentment can cause you unnecessary financial stress and may hold you back from achieving your goals. Letting go of these resentments is key to ending your financial stress.

Relationship-Based Financial Resentment

Because relationship-based financial resentments are as diverse and idiosyncratic as human relationships, discussing financial resentment in respect to personal relationships is something that is too broad for the scope of this book. However, even though we will not be exploring relationship-based financial resentment in depth, the thought exercises provided later in this chapter can help individuals who feel such resentment to let go of their corrosive anger. We will then discuss resentment of larger economic problems in the remainder of this chapter.

Before we start our discussion of economy-based financial resentment, it is important to note that financial resentment within a relationship can sometimes be a warning sign for financial abuse—and financial abuse cannot be solved by letting go of your resentment. If you are experiencing financial resentment within a personal relationship and suspect that you may be in a financially abusive relationship, read through the following list of financial abuse red flags, appearing here courtesy of the website Domestic Shelters (www.domesticshelters.org). Though this list is specifically geared toward marital or romantic relationships, please note that these markers for financial abuse can apply to nearly any personal relationship.

FINANCIAL ABUSE RED FLAGS

Does your partner or loved one do any of the following?

- Forbid you from working?
- Sabotage your employment opportunities?
- Control how money is spent?
- Deny you direct access to bank accounts?
- Give you an "allowance"?
- Force you to write bad checks or file fraudulent tax returns?
- Run up large debts on joint accounts without your permission?
- Force you to work in the family business without pay?
- Refuse to pay bills for accounts that are in your name in order to ruin your credit?
- Force you to turn over paychecks or public benefits checks?
- Force you to account for all money you spend by showing receipts?
- Apply for credit accounts using your name and personal information?
- Withhold money for basic necessities like food, clothing, medication, and housing?
- Spend money on himself or herself but not allow you to do the same?
- Give you presents or pay for things and expect something in return?
- Force you to work while he or she does not and he or she still controls all the money?

If reading through these warning signs makes you suspect that you may be the victim of financial abuse, you can contact the National Domestic Violence Hotline at 800-799-SAFE for advice and next steps. For further reading on the subject of financial abuse in all manner of relationships, I also highly recommend the book *Gold Diggers and Deadbeat Dads: True Stories of Friends, Family, and Financial Ruin* by Valerie Rind.

Financial Resentment of Economy-Wide Problems

For several years, I was a member of a local freelancers' group that met quarterly to share leads and talk shop. At one meeting, a colleague (whom I'll call Joe) and I chatted about how to handle preretirement stress. Joe was in his late fifties and intended to retire within the next seven to ten years, and he was stressed that someone in his social circle had done everything wrong financially but because of a lucky break was on track to retire at about the same time Joe would. Joe, on the other hand, had worked diligently and followed the rules, but had been downsized from his company when the recession hit, and he was late in his career. With few opportunities available to him, Joe turned to freelancing to keep his career going and save enough money to eventually retire.

My colleague had good reason to be angry. Joe had worked hard for his employer, had been responsible with his money and his career, and had ended up getting the short end of the stick in the financial recession of 2008. The acquaintance who had landed on his feet, however, had squandered money and wasted opportunities but lucked into some financial success and learned nothing from his irresponsibility.

Such stories are incredibly common, and they can range from the very impersonal resentment of where your tax dollars go while you struggle to make ends meet to the more specific resentment of individuals you know who are doing better than you financially.

Many of the resentments that people feel over such economic injustices are both perfectly valid and completely justified. Money offers power to those who hold a great deal of it, and American history is full of heartbreaking stories of the rich and powerful maintaining their status on the backs of those less fortunate. We cannot help but feel outraged when hard work does not seem to offer financial reward, despite the fact that the American dream we have all been promised says otherwise.

The problem with such resentment is that it does nothing to improve your situation or bring about true economic justice. As many wise people have said, "Resentment is like swallowing poison and expecting the other person to die."

Specifically, resentment over larger economic problems can cause you to sabotage your own finances in several ways:

GIVING UP THE POSSIBILITY OF GETTING AHEAD

Author Linda Tirado wrote a viral blog post for Huffington Post in 2013, entitled "This Is Why Poor People's Bad Decisions Make Perfect Sense." In it, she explains that she makes many poor financial decisions. "None of them matter, in the long term. I will never not be poor, so what does it matter if I don't pay a thing and a half this week instead of just one thing? It's not like the sacrifice will result in improved circumstances."

Tirado's lack of interest in getting ahead is partially attributable to the scarcity mindset we discussed back in Chapter 4, but it is also a common reaction to financial resentment. The thinking goes that it is impossible to get ahead in a rigged system, so why bother to even try?

WANTING TO PUNISH THOSE YOU DEEM RESPONSIBLE FOR THE INJUSTICE

Seeking punishment for those who have wronged you is a common and natural reaction to resentment, and it is the rational course of action in some cases. For instance, lawsuits can potentially provide both financial restitution and a sense of justice to the wronged parties.

However, financial resentment can often lead to self-sabotaging behavior in the name of punishing those responsible for your predicament. For instance, feeling resentment about how government spends tax money may lead voters to elect candidates who will work against the voters' financial self-interest. Similarly, some individuals might refuse needed help from the government or from corporations because of how they feel about those offering the help. In both cases, resentment causes people to cut off their noses to spite their faces.

OVERSPENDING

Spending money you can't afford is a major financial problem with many causes, including resentment. If you feel resentful that you do not have the resources that others have, you may overspend in order to compensate for those feelings of resentment. You might think that it is unfair that they do not have to worry about money, but at least you can wear the same clothes, drive the same car, attend the same school, or otherwise rub shoulders with them. It can feel as though that kind of spending will prove that you are worthy. Of course, this behavior causes you even more worries about money.

How to Let Go of Financial Resentment

Releasing the resentment you feel is no easy feat. Not only does resentment build upon itself as you look for new things to resent, but the righteousness you feel while in the grip of resentment can be very satisfying. Though it may not be possible to completely rid yourself of financial resentment, you can learn the behavior patterns necessary to let go of such resentment. The following thought exercises can help you do this:

MENTALLY SWITCH PLACES

When my colleague Joe laid out to me all the ways that he was feeling stress over the unfairness of his shaky financial situation as compared to that of his lucky acquaintance, I asked him this question: "Would you switch places with him?"

This is a thought exercise for dealing with envy, but it can work just as well for resentment. When you feel financial resentment because someone who you feel is less worthy than you is achieving or receiving more than you, it's not an apples-to-apples comparison. You are thinking of his life in terms of the one thing he has that you do not. However, life is not a buffet, and it is not possible to switch out a single aspect of someone else's life with your own. Would you really prefer to have all of the other person's problems, weaknesses, and trials just because of the injustice that has been dealt to you?

I asked Joe if he would prefer to have lucked into a secure retirement like his friend, without having worked for it or learned anything from his successes and mistakes. Though Joe's finances were unfairly similar to someone who had made nothing but mistakes, at least Joe could retire knowing he was capable of building a retirement for himself no matter the circumstances. He could feel great satisfaction knowing that he would have been fine no matter what. He did not have to rely on a lucky break to retire. Joe's financial life was unfair, but he had made something with it that he could be proud of. His acquaintance could make no such claim nor derive any such pride from his own financial good fortune.

ASK WHAT'S IN IT FOR YOU

Resentment is a harmful emotion, and yet we all get something out of feeling it. For instance, we often displace our own anger at ourselves or our own feelings of vulnerability by holding on to resentment of another person. This is why it is a good idea to dig into your feelings of resentment to determine what you are getting out of them. Author Caroline Rushforth writes on the website mindbodygreen (www.mindbodygreen.com) that people in the grip of resentment should complete the following sentences to figure out what their resentment is shielding them from:

It is useful for me to feel resentment toward _____ because _____.

To be able to let go of this resentment toward _____ I would need to _____.

If I allow myself to release this resentment, I will _____.
If I do not release this resentment, _____.

RECOGNIZE THE STORY YOU HAVE CREATED

As we discussed at the beginning of this chapter, resentment stems from real or imagined injustices. Oftentimes, the incidents or situations that we resent are occurring entirely within our own heads, and the people we believe are committing injustices against us have intended us no harm. The reason we can resent something that never happened is because we all make up stories in order to assign meaning to our lives. We are especially vulnerable to our own stories that explain why something bad has happened.

For instance, let's say that you notice that your parents always pay for dinner on the rare occasions when you all go out to eat with your brother, but they let you pick up the check when it's just the three of you dining. You might tell yourself the story that your parents have always favored your brother and that they are showing their favoritism by paying for his dinners but not yours. But your parents may be allowing you to pick up the tab because they are proud of your independence and financial savvy. Allowing you to pay for them is a sign of respect they give you, which they do not give to your brother, whom they still consider to be childlike. Without discussing the issue with them, you will never know why they engage in this financial behavior, which will further entrench the story you are telling yourself.

This is why shame researcher Dr. Brené Brown suggests in her book *Rising Strong* that you should complete the sentence, "The story I'm making up is . . ." when you find yourself feeling resentful. Recognizing that you are making up a story can often be enough for you to realize what assumptions are at the root of your resentment. Even if you cannot ask the person you resent if your assumptions are true, merely recognizing that there could be alternative explanations for the issue can allow you to let go of your anger and resentment.

What Forgiveness Is and What It Isn't

Letting go of resentment is ultimately about forgiveness. One of the common misconceptions about forgiveness is that it is the same as condoning the behavior you need to forgive. However, forgiveness is actually about releasing yourself from self-destructive and painful resentment. It is a gift you give to yourself, rather than the person you forgive. You are worthy of a life that is free of resentment, whether or not the person, institution, or situation you resent is worthy of your forgiveness.

Chapter Thirteen Takeaways

1. Financial resentment not only leaves us vulnerable to self-sabotaging and disordered financial behavior, it also tends to grow over time if we do not work to let it go.

2. You may feel financial resentment based on a specific relationship or based on a larger economic problem that affects many people.

3. Relationship-based financial resentments can sometimes be indicators of financial abuse, which cannot be solved through forgiveness.

4. Financial resentment can lead to abandonment of financial goals, self-defeating punishment of those you resent, and overspending to make up for injustices.

5. You can mitigate the effects of financial resentment by imagining that you switched places with the person you resent, by recognizing the benefit you gain from feeling resentful, and by asking yourself what assumptions you are making about the situation you resent.

Conclusion: There Is a Path Out of Financial Stress

When I was a teenager, my mother often liked to remind me that the only thing I had complete control over in my life was my reaction to it. No matter what life handed to me, how I reacted to it was up to me—and I could choose to be positive or negative.

This advice garnered some pretty epic eye rolls at the time, not to mention a few slammed bedroom doors. (Sorry about that, Mom!)

As frustrated as I was by her comments when I was a kid, though, I come back to Mom's advice over and over again as an adult. Life hands out what it hands out, including money. This means money ebbs and flows in ways that seem both unfair and mercurial. We have a choice in how we react to that fact: We can sit with our resentment, our sadness, our anger, and our stress, or we can improve the situation as best we can. It's a choice between saying, "Them's the breaks, and I'll never get ahead!" or "Them's the breaks, so what can I do to make my life better within this situation?"

Forging a path out of financial stress is not an easy thing to do. It takes work to examine your money beliefs, recognize your strengths and weaknesses, align your money choices with your values, resist temptations, ignore financially stressful social pressures, keep track of your money, and pick yourself up when you stumble. It takes a lot less effort to wring your hands or shake your fist at the sky.

This is why advice like my mother's is so often met with rolled eyes; we all want life to be fair and easy at the same time.

But money problems and economic setbacks are a fact of life, whether you're wringing your hands or forging a path. By committing to do the work necessary to change your money mindset, you can keep such problems and setbacks from being more than bumps in the road—which makes the work all worth it.

Changing how you react to money may not be an easy path, but it is the only way to end financial stress. Why not get started right now?

Further Reading

Each of the following books offers more insights into the topics discussed in this book. I have read each of these books and I highly recommend them.

Ariely, Dan. *Predictably Irrational: The Hidden Forces That Shape Our Decisions.* **New York: Harper, 2008.**

Dan Ariely's book is a fascinating examination of all the ways our brains betray us even while we congratulate ourselves on our smart thinking. Ariely is a behavioral economist who conducted many rigorous experiments to reach his conclusions about our irrational brains. His writing style is both humorous and accessible, and this book offers a great deal of insight into your money decisions. I also appreciate the guidance Ariely provides on ways to avoid the logic traps his experiments have illuminated.

Birken, Emily Guy. *The 5 Years Before You Retire: Retirement Planning When You Need It the Most.* **Avon, MA: Adams Media, 2014.**

Birken, Emily Guy. *Choose Your Retirement: Find the Right Path to Your New Adventure.* **Avon, MA: Adams Media, 2015.**

It feels a little odd to recommend my own books to you, but each of these previous titles offer some advice that I was not able to cover within this book. Specifically, *The 5 Years Before You Retire* offers actionable advice on finding a financial adviser and planning for retirement, while *Choose Your Retirement* offers some financial stress-reducing advice for those who feel retirement-related financial stress.

Duhigg, Charles. *The Power of Habit: Why We Do What We Do in Life and Business.* **New York: Random House, 2012.**

The changes you need to make in order to achieve a stress-free financial life often have more to do with habits than choices. Charles Duhigg's *The Power of Habit* will help you understand the science behind habits, and it will teach you how to replace bad habits with good ones. (Unfortunately, there is no way to destroy a bad habit, according to Duhigg's research—you can only replace an established habit with a different one.)

Klontz, Brad, Ted Klontz, and Rick Kahler. *Wired for Wealth: Change the Money Mindsets That Keep You Trapped and Unleash Your Wealth Potential.* **Deerfield Beach, FL: Health Communications, 2009.**

Klontz, et al. dig deep into the psychology of money in this book. You will recall from Chapter 7 that Dr. Brad Klontz is the financial psychologist who coined the term "money scripts." In this book, he and his coauthors offer more insight into money scripts and how they are formed, as well as methods for changing your financial comfort zone, and ways to deal with clashing money scripts in relationships.

Mullainathan, Sendhil, and Eldar Shafir. *Scarcity: The New Science of Having Less and How It Defines Our Lives.* **New York: Picador/Henry Holt and Company, 2014.**

We discussed this book at length in Chapter 4, and I highly recommend that anyone who is experiencing a scarcity mindset read through it. Mullainathan and Shafir lay out convincing arguments as to how our decision-making is limited by the various forms of scarcity we may be living with. This book will help you to both forgive yourself for slipups made on the scarcity mindset and think through actionable methods to improve your situation of scarcity.

Ramsey, Dave. *The Financial Peace Planner: A Step-by-Step Guide to Restoring Your Family's Financial Health.* **New York: Penguin Books, 1998.**

There are many budgeting books out there, but I believe Dave Ramsey's budgeting suggestions are some of the best for working within your psychology and avoiding cognitive bias traps. This is the budgeting book my husband and I used early in our marriage to align our two disparate money mindsets in order to produce a unified budget. The book offers worksheets and exercises to fill out, and it is geared toward married or cohabitating couples. One important caveat about Dave Ramsey: While I have nothing but respect for his budgeting and get-out-of-debt advice, I think his investing advice is wildly optimistic—at best. Get your investment advice elsewhere.

Rind, Valerie. *Gold Diggers and Deadbeat Dads: True Stories of Friends, Family, and Financial Ruin.* **Washington, DC: VSJ Enterprises, 2014.**

Financial abuse is a serious problem that is often swept under the rug. Attorney Valerie Rind personally experienced financial abuse when her (now ex) husband lied to her for years about money. After piecing her financial life back together, Rind decided to research the topic of financial abuse by interviewing victims of financially abusive friends, spouses, lovers, and family members. She not only breaks down the many faces of financial abuse, but she offers advice on how to avoid falling victim to such abuse.

Robin, Vicki, Joseph R. Dominguez, and Monique Tilford. *Your Money or Your Life: 9 Steps to Transforming Your Relationship with Money and Achieving Financial Independence.* **New York: Penguin Books, 2008.**

Author Joe Dominguez retired from paid work when he was thirty-one years old by following the nine steps outlined in this book. He taught others how to achieve financial independence, including Vicki Robin, who has continued the work since Dominguez's death in 1997. Reading *Your Money or Your Life* is a transformational experience that helps you understand just how important it is to align your values with your money choices. Some of Dominguez's original suggestions have become rather dated. Specifically, the investment strategies both Dominguez and Robin used to retire in their thirties will no longer offer a return that could lead to financial independence. Despite that, this book is an excellent read for challenging your assumptions and changing your relationship with money.

Schwartz, Barry. *The Paradox of Choice: Why More Is Less*. New York: Ecco, 2004.
Barry Schwartz explains in *The Paradox of Choice* why living with abundant choice causes us to feel unhappy. Reading through this book will help you better understand ways to increase your life satisfaction by voluntarily reducing your choices and accepting a level of good enough. It has been more than ten years since I first read this book, and I am still using the insights I gained from it on a regular basis.

Szuchman, Paula, and Jenny Anderson. *It's Not You, It's the Dishes: How to Minimize Conflict and Maximize Happiness in Your Relationship*. New York: Random House, 2012.
Though it is nominally a relationship guide, *It's Not You, It's the Dishes* is the most concise and straightforward introduction to the basic principles of economics you'll find. Authors Paula Szuchman and Jenny Anderson provide an excellent introduction to ten different principles from the field of economics, and in each chapter they apply one of these economic theories to marital relationships. The stated purpose of the book is to help the listener improve his or her relationship, but I found that the detailed and well-written explanation of economic principles, along with the micro-examples of how these principles play out in a marriage, helped me to better understand how all groups handle scarce resources. It also helped me to think about the ways I make decisions in every sphere of my life.

Thaler, Richard H., and Cass R. Sunstein. *Nudge: Improving Decisions about Health, Wealth, and Happiness*. New York: Penguin Books, 2009.
Thaler and Sunstein coined the term "choice architecture" in this book, and they explain that the way choices are offered to people can influence which decisions are most likely. For instance, a cafeteria trying to sell more healthy food could place the apples at eye level and put the potato chips on a high shelf. Reading this book can help you understand the ways—both benign and nefarious—that your choices are being made for you.

Twist, Lynne, and Teresa Barker. *The Soul of Money: Reclaiming the Wealth of Our Inner Resources*. New York: W.W. Norton, 2006.
Author Lynne Twist asks her readers to examine the role of culture in their understanding of money. Many of the truths about money that we take as

self-evident actually stem from a culture that is obsessed with money. Twist worked as a fundraiser and representative for The Hunger Project, and she spent a great deal of time in very poor parts of the world, which led her to adjust her attitude toward money. It is her goal that every reader will consider the real-world consequences of their attitudes toward money and resources.

Vanderkam, Laura. *All the Money in the World: What the Happiest People Know about Wealth*. New York: Penguin Books, 2012.
Laura Vanderkam starts *All the Money in the World* with the surprising idea that it is possible to buy happiness. You just need to figure out what would change about your life if you had all the money in the world, and then manage your finances so that you can afford that change. Vanderkam offers suggestions for ways to alter your financial mindset and behavior so that you can live as if you had all the money in the world, but it is clear that she is writing for middle class and upper middle class readers. Nonetheless, her thought exercises can be illuminating for readers anywhere on the income spectrum.

In addition to these sources, the following were consulted in preparing this book:

"10 Warnings When Consolidating Credit Card Debt." Consolidated Credit. www.consolidatedcredit.org/credit-card-debt/credit-card-consolidation/warnings-when-consolidating-credit/.

American Psychological Association. "Stress In America: Paying with Our Health." News release. February 4, 2015. APA. www.apa.org/news/press/releases/stress/2014/stress-report.pdf.

"Are You the Victim of Financial Abuse?" Domestic Shelters. June 12, 2015. www.domesticshelters.org/domestic-violence-articles-information/are-you-the-victim-of-financial-abuse.

Babauta, Leo. "15 Great Decluttering Tips." Zen Habits. October 24, 2007. https://zenhabits.net/15-great-decluttering-tips/.

Balls, Andrew. "The Path of Least Resistance in 401(k) Plans." National Bureau of Economic Research. April 2002. www.nber.org/digest/apr02/w8651.html.

Beck, Martha. "The Cure for Self-Consciousness." Oprah.com. July 2007. www.oprah.com/spirit/Martha-Becks-Cure-for-Self-Consciousness.

Becker, Joshua. "A Helpful Guide to Overcoming Envy." *Becoming Minimalist*. September 2015. www.becomingminimalist.com/ungreen-with-envy/.

Birken, Emily Guy. "3 Scientific Ways to Psych Yourself Up for a Job
   Interview." MoneyNing. June 2015. http://moneyning.com/
   career/3-scientific-ways-to-psych-yourself-up-for-a-job-interview/.

Birken, Emily Guy. "3 Times When You Should Absolutely Quit." Wise Bread. May
   28, 2015. www.wisebread.com/3-times-when-you-should-absolutely-quit.

Birken, Emily Guy. "Adjust Your W4 to Maximize Your Take-Home Pay
   This Year." MoneyNing. January 2012. http://moneyning.com/tax/
   adjust-your-w4-to-maximize-your-take-home-pay-this-year/.

Birken, Emily Guy. "Are You Letting FOMO Ruin Your Finances?" Wise Bread. March
   10, 2016. www.wisebread.com/are-you-letting-fomo-ruin-your-finances.

Birken, Emily Guy. "Are You a Maximizer or a Satisficer?" Live Like a Mensch.
   January 2013. http://community.stretcher.com/blogs/live_like_a_mensch/
   archive/2013/01/15/are-you-a-maximizer-or-a-satisficer.aspx.

Birken, Emily Guy. "Avoid Buyer's Remorse: Use These Psychological Tricks to
   Spend Money Wisely." PT Money. January 2013. https://ptmoney.com/
   psychological-tricks-to-avoid-buyers-remorse/.

Birken, Emily Guy. "The Best Automatic Savings Apps (to Grow Your Wealth in 2016)."
   PT Money. January 2016. https://ptmoney.com/best-automatic-savings-apps/.

Birken, Emily Guy. "The Best Personal Finance Software for Taming Your
   Budget (in 2016)." PT Money. June 2016. https://ptmoney.com/
   best-personal-finance-software/.

Birken, Emily Guy. "Bigger Paycheck or Bigger Tax Refund—Which Should
   You Pick?" Wise Bread. March 31, 2015. www.wisebread.com/
   bigger-paycheck-or-bigger-tax-refund-which-should-you-pick.

Birken, Emily Guy. "How Anchoring in Behavioral Economics Explains Your Irrational
   Money Choices." MoneyNing. October 2011. http://moneyning.com/
   money-beliefs/how-anchoring-in-behavioral-economics-explains-your-
   irrational-money-choices/.

Birken, Emily Guy. "How Availability Heuristic in Behavioral Economics Explains
   Your Irrational Money Choices." MoneyNing. November 2011. http://
   moneyning.com/money-beliefs/how-availability-heuristic-in-behavioral-
   economics-explains-your-irrational-money-choices/.

Birken, Emily Guy. "How Hyperbolic Discounting in Behavioral Economics
   Explains Your Irrational Money Choices." MoneyNing. November 2011.
   http://moneyning.com/money-beliefs/how-hyperbolic-discounting-in-
   behavioral-economics-explains-your-irrational-money-choices/.

Birken, Emily Guy. "How Loss Aversion in Behavioral Economics Explains Your Irrational Money Choices." MoneyNing. October 2011. http://moneyning.com/money-beliefs/how-loss-aversion-in-behavioral-economics-explains-your-irrational-money-choices/.

Birken, Emily Guy. "How Much Money Can You Be Responsible For?" *Live Like a Mensch.* May 6, 2015. http://social.stretcher.com/blogs/12/300/how-much-money-can-you-be-respon.

Birken, Emily Guy. "How to Increase Willpower and Stay on Track Financially." PT Money. May 2013. https://ptmoney.com/how-to-increase-willpower/.

Birken, Emily Guy. *Making Social Security Work for You: Advice, Strategies, and Timelines That Can Maximize Your Benefits.* Avon, MA: Adams Media, 2016.

Birken, Emily Guy. "Mental Accounting: Why You Blow Your Tax Refund but Not Your Raise." Wise Bread. March 12, 2013. www.wisebread.com/mental-accounting-why-you-blow-your-tax-refund-but-not-your-raise.

Birken, Emily Guy. "Trim Review: Cancel Your Forgotten Subscriptions." PT Money. April 2016. https://ptmoney.com/trim-review/.

Birken, Emily Guy. "What Did Your Parents REALLY Teach You about Money? (It Might Surprise You)." Wise Bread. June 12, 2014. www.wisebread.com/what-did-your-parents-really-teach-you-about-money-it-might-surprise-you.

Birken, Emily Guy. "Why It May Cost You More When It's Free." PT Money. February 2013. https://ptmoney.com/why-it-may-cost-you-more-when-its-free/.

Birken, Emily Guy. "Why *Should* Is a Dangerous Word." *Live Like a Mensch.* August 24, 2012. http://community.stretcher.com/blogs/live_like_a_mensch/archive/2012/08/24/why-should-is-a-dangerous-word.aspx.

Birken, Emily Guy. "Why We Spend More When We Pay with Credit Cards." Wise Bread. October 23, 2012. www.wisebread.com/why-we-spend-more-when-we-pay-with-credit-cards.

Birken, Emily Guy. "Your Ultimate Guide to Credit Card Consolidation | Student Loan Hero." Student Loan Hero. June 13, 2016. https://studentloanhero.com/featured/credit-card-consolidation-guide/.

Bissonnette, Zac. "Half of Americans Can't Raise $2K in 30 Days | TIME.com." Time. June 1, 2011. http://business.time.com/2011/06/01/nearly-half-of-americans-would-struggle-to-come-up-with-2k-in-30-days/.

Brickman, Philip, Dan Coates, and Ronnie Janoff-Bulman. "Lottery Winners and Accident Victims: Is Happiness Relative?" *Journal of Personality and Social Psychology* 36, no. 8 (August 1978): 917–27. doi:10.1037/0022-3514.36.8.917.

Chatterjee, Promothesh. "Payment Methods Affect Consumers' Perceptions of Products." Phys.org. January 26, 2016. http://phys.org/news/2016-01-payment-methods-affect-consumers-perceptions.html.

Cherry, Kendra. "What Is a Cognitive Bias? Definition and Examples." Verywell. May 9, 2016. https://www.verywell.com/what-is-a-cognitive-bias-2794963.

"Clean Freaks." *Newsweek.* June 6, 2004. www.newsweek.com/clean-freaks-129009.

Crary, Mindy. "15 Ways to Improve Your Relationship with Money." *Forbes.* February 13, 2012. www.forbes.com/sites/moneywisewomen/2012/02/13/15-ways-to-improve-your-relationship-with-money/.

Dew, Jeffrey, Sonya Britt, and Sandra Huston. "Examining the Relationship Between Financial Issues and Divorce." *Family Relations* 61, no. 4 (2012): 615–28. doi:10.1111/j.1741-3729.2012.00715.x.

Doody, Ryan. "The Sunk Cost 'Fallacy' Is Not a Fallacy." PhD diss., MIT, 2013. November 1, 2013. www.mit.edu/~rdoody/TheSunkCostFallacy.pdf.

Dunning, David. "Science AMA Series." Reddit. November 13, 2014. https://www.reddit.com/r/science/comments/2m6d68/science_ama_seriesim_david_dunning_a_social/.

Dynarski, Susan, and Judith Scott-Clayton. "There Is a Simpler Way for Students to Apply for Financial Aid." *The New York Times.* June 20, 2014. www.nytimes.com/2014/06/21/upshot/a-simple-way-to-help-financial-aid-do-its-job.html.

"The Economic Impact of Grey Charges on Debit and Credit Card Issuers." Aite Group. July 25, 2013. http://aitegroup.com/report/economic-impact-grey-charges-debit-and-credit-card-issuers.

Emmons, Robert. "The New Science of Gratitude." Gratitude Power. http://gratitudepower.net/science.htm.

Emmons, Robert. "Why Gratitude Is Good." Greater Good. November 16, 2010. http://greatergood.berkeley.edu/article/item/why_gratitude_is_good/.

"Form W-4 and Your Take-Home Pay." TurboTax. https://turbotax.intuit.com/tax-tools/tax-tips/Jobs-and-Career/Form-W-4-and-Your-Take-Home-Pay/INF12026.html.

Friend, Tad. "Jumpers: The Fatal Grandeur of the Golden Gate Bridge." *New Yorker*. October 13, 2003. www.newyorker.com/magazine/2003/10/13/jumpers.

Furman, Grace. "A Simple Phrase That Can Prevent Arguments and Resentment." Tiny Buddha. http://tinybuddha.com/blog/ a-simple-phrase-that-can-prevent-arguments-and-resentment/.

Gailliot, Matthew T., Roy F. Baumeister, C. Nathan Dewall, Jon K. Maner, E. Ashby Plant, Dianne M. Tice, Lauren E. Brewer, and Brandon J. Schmeichel. "Self-Control Relies on Glucose As a Limited Energy Source: Willpower Is More Than a Metaphor." *Journal of Personality and Social Psychology* 92, no. 2 (2007): 325–36. doi:10.1037/0022-3514.92.2.325.

Hancock, Adam M., Bryce L. Jorgensen, and Melvin S. Swanson. "College Students and Credit Card Use: The Role of Parents, Work Experience, Financial Knowledge, and Credit Card Attitudes." *Journal of Family and Economic Issues* 34, no. 4 (2013): 369–81. doi:10.1007/s10834-012-9338-8.

Harden, Seth. "Gym Membership Statistics." Statistic Brain. December 1, 2015. www.statisticbrain.com/gym-membership-statistics/.

Henry, Alan. "Productivity 101: A Primer to the Getting Things Done (GTD) Philosophy." *Lifehacker*. March 26, 2014. http://lifehacker.com/ productivity-101-a-primer-to-the-getting-things-done-1551880955.

Hershfield, Hal E. "The Way We Spend Impacts How We Spend." *Psychology Today*. July 10, 2012. https://www.psychologytoday.com/blog/ the-edge-choice/201207/the-way-we-spend-impacts-how-we-spend.

Hipsher, Bill. "Storage 101: Pricing of Self Storage." Storage Talk. April 5, 2013. http://blog.storage.com/pricing-of-self-storage/.

Holland, Kelley. "The Downside of Automatic 401(k) Enrollment." CNBC. June 29, 2015. www.cnbc.com/2015/06/29/the-downside-of-automatic-401k-enrollment.html.

"The Importance of Gratitude." University of Massachusetts Dartmouth. https://www.umassd.edu/counseling/forparents/reccomendedreadings/ theimportanceofgratitude/.

Johnson, Holly. "Six Bills You Can Negotiate Down to Save Money." The Simple Dollar. www.thesimpledollar.com/six-bills-you-can-negotiate-down/.

Karlan, Dean S., and Jonathan Morduch. *Microeconomics*. New York: McGraw-Hill Education, 2015.

Klontz, Brad, and Ted Klontz. "Top 10 Money Scripts That Mess-Up People's Financial Lives." Your Mental Wealth. May 5, 2009. www.yourmentalwealth.com/top-10-money-scripts-that-mess-up-peoples-financial-lives/.

Konnikova, Maria. "No Money, No Time." The New York Times. June 13, 2014, Opinionator sec. June 13, 2014. http://opinionator.blogs.nytimes.com/2014/06/13/no-clocking-out/.

Lacy, Lisa. "How to Negotiate for a Better Cell Phone Bill." LearnVest. May 11, 2010. www.learnvest.com/knowledge-center/how-to-negotiate-for-a-better-cell-phone-bill/.

Lambert, Craig. "The Marketplace of Perceptions." Harvard Magazine. March/April 2006. http://harvardmagazine.com/2006/03/the-marketplace-of-perce.html.

Lusardi, Annamaria, Daniel Schneider, and Peter Tufano. "Financially Fragile Households: Evidence and Implications." National Bureau of Economic Research, May 2011. doi:10.3386/w17072.

McCormally, Kevin. "How to Keep Your Tax Refund Safe (and Get Paid to Do It)." Kiplinger. January 21, 2016. www.kiplinger.com/article/taxes/T056-C000-S001-one-simple-trick-to-fraud-proof-your-tax-refund.html.

Ormrod, J.E. "Problem-Solving Strategies: Algorithms and Heuristics." Education.com. July 20, 2010. www.education.com/reference/article/problem-solving-strategies-algorithms/.

Passuello, Luciano. "Sunk Cost Bias: How It Hinders Your Life and 4 Ways to Overcome It." Litemind. 2011. https://litemind.com/sunk-cost-bias/.

Prelec, Drazen, and George Loewenstein. "The Red and the Black: Mental Accounting of Savings and Debt." Marketing Science 17, no. 1 (1998): 4–28. doi:10.1287/mksc.17.1.4.

Raghubir, Priya, and Joydeep Srivastava. The Denomination Effect. NYU Stern School of Business. January 2009. http://w4.stern.nyu.edu/news/docs/Denomination_Round_4-1.pdf.

Renzulli, Kerri Anne. "7 Tips for Slashing Your Cable Bill from Guys Who Do It for a Living." Time. March 21, 2016. http://time.com/money/4253989/cut-cable-bills-tips-tricks/.

"Resistance Training for Your 'Willpower' Muscles." NPR. September 18, 2011. www.npr.org/2011/09/18/140516974/resistance-training-for-your-willpower-muscles.

Roth, J.D. "How to Use Barriers and Pre-Commitment to Automatically Do the Right Thing." *Money Boss.* December 10, 2015. http://moneyboss.com/how-to-use-barriers-and-pre-commitment-to-automatically-do-the-right-thing/.

Rushforth, Caroline. "How to Let Go of Resentment." Mindbodygreen. November 9, 2012. www.mindbodygreen.com/0-6778/How-to-Let-Go-of-Resentment.html.

Sahadi, Jeanne. "Nearly 8 Out of 10 U.S. Tax Filers Get Tax Refunds." CNNMoney. January 14, 2015. http://money.cnn.com/2015/01/13/pf/taxes/taxpayer-refunds/index.html.

Schwartz, Barry, Andrew Ward, John Monterosso, Sonja Lyubomirsky, Katherine White, and Darrin R. Lehman. "Maximizing versus Satisficing: Happiness Is a Matter of Choice." *Journal of Personality and Social Psychology* 83, no. 5 (May 2, 2002): 1178–197. doi:10.1037/0022-3514.83.5.1178.

Selig, Meg. "Beware the 'What-the-Hell Effect,' Especially on Holidays!" *Psychology Today.* November 21, 2011. https://www.psychologytoday.com/blog/changepower/201111/beware-the-what-the-hell-effect-especially-holidays.

Sethi, Ramit. "Barriers Are Your Enemy." *I Will Teach You to Be Rich.* www.iwillteachyoutoberich.com/blog/barriers-are-your-enemy/.

Sethi, Ramit. "The Psychology of Passive Barriers: Why Your Friends Don't Save Money, Eat Healthier, or Clean Their Garages." Get Rich Slowly. March 17, 2009. www.getrichslowly.org/blog/2009/03/17/the-psychology-of-passive-barriers-why-your-friends-dont-save-money-eat-healthier-or-clean-their-garages/.

Smith, Anne Kates. "Your Worst Money Problems Are All in Your Head." *Kiplinger.* July 31, 2012. www.kiplinger.com/article/spending/T031-C000-S002-your-worst-money-problems-are-all-in-your-head.html.

Stosny, Steven. "Chains of Resentment." *Psychology Today.* September 9, 2011. https://www.psychologytoday.com/blog/anger-in-the-age-entitlement/201109/chains-resentment.

Sunstein, Cass R. "It Captures Your Mind." *New York Review of Books.* September 26, 2013. www.nybooks.com/articles/2013/09/26/it-captures-your-mind/.

"Tax Refunds Reach Almost $125 Billion Mark; IRS.gov Available for Tax Help." IRS. February 26, 2015. https://www.irs.gov/uac/newsroom/tax-refunds-reach-almost-125-billion-mark-irs-gov-available-for-tax-help.

Thaler, Richard H. "Mental Accounting Matters." *Journal of Behavioral Decision Making* 12, no. 3 (1999): 183–206. doi:10.1002/(sici)1099-0771(199909)12:33.0.co;2-f.

Tirado, Linda. "This Is Why Poor People's Bad Decisions Make Perfect Sense." Huffington Post. November 22, 2013. www.huffingtonpost.com/linda-tirado/ why-poor-peoples-bad-decisions-make-perfect-sense_b_4326233.html.

"U.S. Commuters Wait Approximately 40 Mins. a Day for Public Transit." Metro. December 11, 2014. www.metro-magazine.com/accessibility/ news/292870/u-s-commuters-wait-approximately-40-mins-a-day-for-public-transit.

"The Upside of Quitting: Full Transcript." Freakonomics. September 30, 2011. http://freakonomics.com/2011/09/30/the-upside-of-quitting-full-transcript/.

Vedantam, Shankar. "Mental Accounting: Why It's Easy to Blow the Tax Refund and Hard to Catch a Cab in the Rain." The Washington Post. May 20, 2007. www.washingtonpost.com/wp-dyn/content/article/2007/05/19/ AR2007051900316.html.

Whitney, Roger P. "LIVE YOU Worksheet: Managing Your Lifestyle." Roger Whitney. February 2014. http://rogerwhitney.com/wp-content/uploads/2014/02/ LIVE-Worksheet-Managing-Lifestyle.pdf.

Yip, Pamela. "How Your 'Money Script' Can Affect Your Finances." Dallas News. May 2013. www.dallasnews.com/business/money/2013/05/31/ how-your-money-script-can-affect-your-finances.

Index

About the Author

Emily Guy Birken is a former educator and a respected personal finance blogger. Her background in education allows her to make complex financial topics relatable and easily understood by the layperson. Her work has appeared on the sites PT Money, Wise Bread, Student Loan Hero, MoneyNing, Huffington Post, and Business Insider, as well as Kiplinger, MSN Money, and The New York Times online. She has also appeared on the Wisconsin Public Radio program Central Time hosted by Rob Ferrett and on The Washington Post's Color of Money Live Chat with Michelle Singletary.

Emily has a bachelor's degree in English with an emphasis in writing from Kenyon College, and a master's degree in education from The Ohio State University. She lives in Milwaukee, Wisconsin, with her husband Jayme, a mechanical engineer, and her two sons Ari and James.